This book is
dedicated to friends
everywhere —
and especially
to those most in need
of them.

TAKING TURNS : conversations in color

Essays by Sylvia Sullivan Villarreal
Paintings by Bonnie J. Brewer

PUBLICATIONS

PUBLICATIONS

Illustrations copyright © 2006 by Bonnie Brewer
Text copyright © 2006 by Sylvia Sullivan Villarreal

Published by
Conversations in Color Publications
Houston, TX
Book Design by Jill Feuk

ISBN 0-9787626-0-6
ISBN 978-0-9787626-0-5
Printed in China

ACKNOWLEDGEMENTS

I believe that it is my whole family and all of my friends who have helped to shape and guide me on my life's journey. Following are a few of these important people.

Sylvia, my inspiring friend who I treasure. Nonnie, Pa, Filomena, Kenneth, Aunt Grayce, Ken, Debbie, Casey, Nell, Jesse, Luke, John, Kim, Chris, Jose, Ruth, Karen, Mac, Sara, Jim, Dee, and Jill Feuk, our patient friend and graphic designer.

Bonnie Brewer

ACKNOWLEDGEMENTS

Aside from Bonnie, whose friendship is one of the finest gifts of my life, and our friend and graphic designer, the multi-talented and refreshingly modest Jill Feuk, who got it just right, there are many people owed thanks around this project. Beginning with the Sullivan clan; our late parents, Ed and Helen and my eight siblings, all their spouses and the gorgeous children who have descended from these unions, right through our newest crop of beautiful grandbabies—you are all the foundation I build upon.

As for just some of the amazing womenfolk in my life: my three sisters, Gay, Suzy, and Deirdre, my early friends Diane and the late, lovely Mary Ann, Susan, Fran, and all of their children, you are each written on my heart. To Patty, Nancy, Melissa, and Harriette, who helped me swim through some murky waters, go my love and thanks. To my colleagues and friends at the Clinic who encouraged and supported my work, my gratitude for listening and caring.

Two of the major teachers in my life are my adult children Miguel and Kate, whose thoughtful, productive lives are a source of unexpected turns and deep pride. And for my spouse and partner in all things, Jose Villarreal, with whom I share all but my DNA, my debt to you is beyond calculation. For consistently overestimating my strengths while generously overlooking my flaws, your belief in the importance of this work has helped make this book happen. For that and for all the ways in which you grace this world, I am so deeply grateful.

Sylvia Sullivan Villarreal

It Is Your Turn Now

It is your turn now,
you waited, you were patient.
The time has come,
for us to polish you.
We will transform your inner pearl
into a house of fire.
You're a gold mine.
Did you know that,
hidden in the dirt of the earth?
It is your turn now,
to be placed in fire.
Let us cremate your impurities.

Reprinted with permission.
From: Hush Don't Say Anything to God:
*   Passionate Poems of Rumi*
Translated by Sharam Shiva

INTRODUCTION

One of the sweetest of life's offerings is the opportunity to bond deeply and joyfully with another human being. Our relationships can take many forms: the rapturous ecstasy that transfixes new lovers, the pure and consuming love of first time parents, the filial devotion of children, the seasoned, mature love of long time partners, and of course, the comforting, tried and true intimacy that develops between long time friends.

It is this last category that frames the content of this book. Thirty nine years of friendship and virtually all of life's significant events are woven into the relationship between the two authors. We met as coworkers and classmates during our college years in the late 1960's, and have remained friends throughout marriages, degrees, births, deaths, cross-country moves, divorce, career changes, major illness, and a host of other things encountered in daily life.

Throughout the good times, and even more critically in the not so good times, our shared history, our almost cellular level of connection and mutual respect has been a refuge, a familiar and safe resting place. In the spaces created by a long and rich friendship, there has always been time for celebrating triumphs, mourning losses, and entertaining the questions that constantly occur in the lives of persons who attempt to live with some degree of awareness. For one of us, written words are the most natural way to handle the tug and pull of all of the emotions that flow through human beings. For the other, using color, texture and the discipline of translating through the hands what is so deeply felt in the soul, is the medium of choice.

In this collaboration, we strive to blend some of our life experiences both as individuals and as friends, using the paintings of the artist as a catalyst for exploring some of the stages, situations, emotions, and challenges that inhabit all of our lives. We claim no special expertise as artist, writer, or in any other arena. Rather we welcome the reader to join us in our dialogue, to linger for awhile in the territory of a friendship, to rejoice in our attempt to fine tune some of the connections between human hearts.

Sylvia Sullivan Villarreal

ARTIST STATEMENT

Painting is my language and its alphabet consists of color, line, shape, value, texture, temperature, and intensity of color. Painting is my way of saying "Yes" to life, for if not now, when?

The experience of embracing painting as my full-time pursuit has been my own version of an "outward bound" adventure. Painting is a highly physical activity in so many ways: whether outside transporting easels, canvases, and supplies to different locations in search of good light, or being at home in my studio, mixing colors and choosing brushes or palette knives. Each time I approach my easel, I risk breaking the rules in order to transfer to the canvas the things that dance in my head. And every time I face a blank canvas, I wrestle anew with my soul.

Whatever media each of us chooses, our creations give voice to life's many lessons. They reflect how our interpretations of these experiences shape us. Developing and expressing my voice through painting is one of the highest honors of being alive. Another pleasure of this project is the chance to dialogue with my lifelong friend Sylvia, whose passion is writing. We have learned more about each other through this project and our processes of communication- their similarities as well as their differences.

It is our joint hope that the reader/viewer of this book is encouraged to find and celebrate their own voice through the medium of their choice.

Bonnie Brewer

TITLES

OUT OF THE BLUE

ACRYLIC   **16" X 20"**

Although the intense colors: blue, red, green are proportionately less than the neutral color field, they help to define and enliven it. This contrast of colors reminds me that when we connect with or rediscover things we are passionate about, our days are reconfigured and invigorated. We step out of ourselves, radiant and enhanced by our life experiences.

L O V E

Bonnie and I first met in the infamous 1960's when "free love" was the slogan of the decade and social conventions were toppling faster than bowling pins in an alley on a Saturday night. Bonnie, tall and slim, inherited her large deep brown eyes and glossy black curls from her Italian mother, and looked like a model. She had the most dazzling smile I had ever seen. The fact that she was elegantly dressed with perfect posture and diction attracted a wide array of people to her. She was nineteen, I was seventeen and we wound up working together in a college library. Despite the fact that I was her polar physical opposite (short, fair-skinned, curvy,) we became instant friends. Somewhere between the polish of her exquisite manners, and my quirky humor, a spark ignited that has never faded. We found out immediately that we both loved to converse, to explore both new ideas and new places, to reflect on and process aloud things that occurred in our lives, and mostly to laugh, often spontaneously and without great reason, just for the sheer joy of it.

As healthy young women we spent lots of time on the topic of true love. We entertained and endured each others romantic attachments and pondered what our lives would hold in this arena. Although "women's lib" was well into vogue, we each came out of a religious and family tradition that posited marriage as the completing event in any woman's life. I think we vaguely pictured ourselves living somewhat creative and free lives, but each with a partner who would most likely be a husband.

And "out of the blue" it happened for us. Bonnie married in May, and I in December of 1972. I was maid of honor for my best friend who had an intimate ceremony in a lovely old church. I married at the college chapel, with guitars strumming and my new husband and I exchanging vows we had written for ourselves and approved by our hip young priest-friend. On to the happily ever after.

We have learned in those thirty plus years that love is a complicated and consuming journey, and its final destination is never certain. While some relationships do a slow and steady simmer, others ignite quickly, filling needs that are not even consciously known in either party. They may go on to a depth and intensity that cannot be imagined by new lovers. Others may initially soar, peak, then flame out in the challenges and minutiae of everyday life. Marriage, for most of us back then when the option of living together was in its infancy, was indeed a leap in the dark. We have since learned that even if the marriage is not forever, one is well advised to honor the courage it takes to make that leap, to learn whatever it is possible to learn from the experience, and then to proceed to do those things that lead to the most inner peace possible for all the parties involved.

As friends we have shared some of the gut wrenching sadness that comes when reality insists that the fantasy will not work out. And more importantly we've learned that, in the school of love, there is no advanced degree that grants and ensures tenure. Unless two people are willing to honestly and openly face their differences and make some concessions in service of the relationship, then all the shoulds and all the longing in the world cannot make things right. We know now that although love indeed often comes "out of the blue" into our lives, once it arrives, it needs care and attention and constant nurturing from both parties to sustain and deepen it.

We have also both lived long enough to understand that what seems to be the end, that dreaded black hole into which all the happiness of one's past life threatens to vanish after the loss of a love, is just another stop along the road. We now know that being able to just sit with all the painful emotions, and to resist the urge to rage and blame ourselves or the other, is the quickest path to recovery. And watching each other as we have attempted to work through difficult situations has been a source of pain and pride for both of us.

Loving another person for your whole life is a monumental task at times. Leaving a relationship, then truly being able to let go, is also the work of a lifetime. Fairy tale endings in life are rare indeed.

Our own friendship is a prototype for the accidental encounter of two people who are thrown together and discover in each other a reflecting pool that allows them the safety to explore some of life's most difficult challenges. One relationship, be it spouse, partner, friend, sibling, cannot satisfy any person's full complement of needs. But one very real and conscious friendship can act as a radar beam for those times when we slowly and inevitably drift off course. And it is such a reassuring place to go when expectations and real life experience turn out to be contradictory. It helps enormously to have someone who knew you before and after, to sort out some of the painful but potentially valuable new knowledge you have likely acquired.

It's a lot like coming home.

PEONIES

ACRYLIC   16" X 20"

I have always found peonies like these to be a wake-up call to our senses. While painting them, I tuned into an awareness of their intoxicating scent, the silky softness of their petals, and the visual feast they create for the eye.

SENSUALITY

For Bonnie, it can be stripping off the sheets and remaking the bed in clean, fragrant linens. Sheets that have blown dry in the fresh air are prime. For me, putting on some classical guitar, and uncorking a good bottle of red wine will do it. Jazz music that emanates from a dimly lit room. A whiff of aftershave lingering after that morning goodbye kiss. In a world often awash in raw and increasingly graphic sexual imagery, the notion of sensuality is akin to that first awareness of a cooling sea breeze that blows away the humidity of a summer afternoon. If we were to ask any person what they find sensual, the results would be as diverse as the respondents.

Unlike the punch of overt sexual imagery, sensuality connotes something much more subtle and innocent. A long, delicious cat stretch. A hand that lingers as it caresses your cheek. Swimming without a suit. Biting into a fat, lusciously ripe strawberry. Salsa dancing with all it's hip swiveling action. Any and all things that surprise, delight, and tickle the senses, just like the sight of these big, sassy, bodacious peonies, spilling over the sides of their container and giving us a glimpse at their innermost surfaces. All evocative, all conscious, all sensual.

In our overly sexualized society the joys of the sensual can easily be overwhelmed, causing a loss of awareness of this vital aspect of our every-day lives. Bonnie and I recently saw a movie together that beautifully illustrated the power of the mundane to communicate a simmering sensuality without any need for overt physical contact. The film was a tale of a Dutch master and his young female assistant, who later became the subject of one of his famous paintings. The film is done in muted tones with lighting that enhances the luminosity of skin and eyes. In one scene the master is instructing his young female assistant in the art of grinding and mixing various substances to make the colors he needs. In the scene the small pots of crimson, azure blue and rich browns are mixed with liquids from various glass decanters of pleasing shapes and sizes. As they work side by side, the sounds of their scraping, pounding, and mixing, the rhythm of their movements, along with the intensity of the glances that pass between them rivet the viewer, drawing us deeper into the unspoken longing that is so powerfully present. This highly sensual encounter is far more provocative than some explicit films featuring full on bodily contact in some anonymous hotel room.

This quality of sensuality, which extends far beyond the sexual, is readily available to us once we tap into aspects of our daily landscapes. My brother-in-law is a shining example of imbuing everyday ritual with sensual awareness. A French teacher and a gourmet cook, he has always had a love affair with the preparation and serving of good food. From market to the final presentation at table, he is conscious and engaged with every step. Watching him prepare a feast is like a crash course in the art of the sensual. Opera is often his musical backdrop as he assembles, washes, preps, chops and seasons. Aromas, the sounds of sizzling pans, the colors and textures of the vegetables, all combine to seduce the onlooker as he works his magic. The same kind of attention goes to the laying of the table which is the staging area for his culinary expressions of abundance. His celebratory meals are rightfully part of our family lore.

Yet even on the everyday table, he can insert something that awakens and pleases the senses, a frosted silver pitcher of juice at brunch, a cucumber carved into a flower on a vegetable tray, this innate enthusiasm for making the everyday extraordinary is his gift to all who come into his sphere. As for the rewards that flow from his embrace of the sensual life, I shall defer those questions to my sister, a decidedly sensuous woman in her own right!

My sisters also have a keen eye for what is pleasing to the senses that is evidenced in their homes and hospitality. My youngest sister, trained as a painter, wields her sense of color with a mastery that makes her home both cozy and stimulating. Her attention to textures and details makes visiting her

a decidedly sensual experience. I have a vivid memory of staying with her during some frosty New England weather and awakening to find her already downstairs and preparing breakfast for me on a tray, filled with bright pottery and a colorful napkin. As we sat in her sunny den, the radiators hissing and banging in the background, she produced a footstool and a fuzzy, warm mohair throw to cover our toes against the morning chill. We talked and caught up, enjoying the freshly squeezed juice, toasted bread and jam, and hot, strong coffee. Under her care, I felt as pampered as any guest at the Ritz Carlton just a few miles away. That scene awakens a moment of real pleasure to this day.

My middle sister is another kind of artist whose medium is her surroundings. She often takes a paintbrush to a room and remakes a whole environment in a day with ease and assurance. Her eyes dance with possibilities when she contemplates a new space and the pleasure she both gets and creates in the transformation is her way of living the sensual life.

Cultivating sensuality in our daily lives brings rewards that deepen over time. A beach picnic at sunset. A long, aromatic bath. Wrapping yourself in that soft, silky robe. Grinding and inhaling the aroma of fresh coffee beans. Digging deeply into fresh, fertile soil. Walking with your face upturned in the rain. Cuddling with a freshly bathed, heavenly scented baby. Running fast and furiously and feeling your heart pound as your legs pump. Belting out a bluesy song. Gyrating to an insistent beat. Listening intently to a performance of the Bolero. (My friend Fran and I joked about needing a cigarette after watching it recently.) The possibilities for experiencing the sensual aspects of life are virtually limitless; all you need is attention and awareness.

From the way light plays on lace curtains blowing at a window to the way a freshly sliced pineapple lies on a plate, there are endless chances to see, hear, taste, touch, and inhale the sensual life. There are so many avenues by which we can be moved and stimulated through our physical senses. From high impact aerobics to slow, close dancing we all possess the ability to experience small pleasures that so often pass unnoticed under the weight of our daily, hurried, lives. And any effort that we exert in cultivating the art of the sensual will only expand our capacity for happiness.

So rather than seeking out that ever pricier restaurant meal or tickets to the most expensive performance in town, try this little experiment. Go to your local grocery store and buy the freshest ingredients you can find for a simple meal. Set a table with things that you love –never mind all those perfectly correct place settings in the magazines- and be sure to treat yourself to some bodacious flowers like the ones in this painting. Invite your dinner companions to bring with them something they might like to share with you; music, a book of poetry, an original piece of writing or art work. Put on some great music and prepare for an evening of conscious awareness. Eat, drink, talk, laugh, disagree, compromise, dance, sing but above all – be present!

In experiencing such an evening you will be reinvigorating your awareness of the sensual life and all the richness it offers. And you will reinforce the habit of creating your world from the inside out, rather than just accepting without question the constant search for newer, bigger, better that drives so much of our current behavior.

In reclaiming the sensual side of life, we really reclaim our selves.

B R A E B U R N   A P P L E

WATERCOLOR   11" X 14"

In painting this apple, I couldn't help but associate it with learning. "An apple for the teacher" was the popular chant of my elementary school days. Even today, this luscious ripe apple remains for me a symbol of lifelong learning, an invitation to all of us to keep reinventing ourselves.

LEARNING

Bonnie and I have a little problem with books. Namely the ones that spill over our nightstands, off the shelves that groan under their weight, and especially the ones that have now sat forlornly in a humid garage for over a decade, currently inhabited by the most exotic of mold spores. Our problem is that we can't seem to get our hands on enough of them, and once we have them, there never seems to be time to devour them all. And as for letting go of them, let's just say that Bonnie is further along that path than I.

We have both been accused of being perpetual students (both of us have returned to graduate school more than once) and merrily continue that tradition today with various forays into a classroom. We're suckers for painting classes, writing workshops, in fact anytime we can sit in a room with other eager people and get inside the brain of somebody we know has something to offer, we tend to get a little excited.

Back in our college days when we worked in the library together, we were fascinated by the titles of various foreign medical journals and would send ourselves into fits of hilarity when we tried to pronounce their names. Our library job was in the Nursing School and we often compared notes on the faculty members, usually finding ourselves drawn to those professors who would challenge their students with a demanding syllabus, and a call to see the material from an alternative perspective.

Luckily for us, our college era was peppered with sit-ins, teach-ins, (and of course the occasional love-ins) and the order of the day was often very loud, sometimes confrontational exchanges of ideas. Though we experienced some of the negatives of the time, like watching brilliant people self-destruct on drugs and political agendas that led some into violent activity, we also had the opportunity to march a little, sing a little, and dabble a little in the experience of the counter culture. We had long and passionate discussions about civil rights, equal rights, and the right of the individual in relation to the whole society. While our time in college was a tumultuous one for the larger society, it was probably ultimately helpful for two well bred Catholic girls needing to enlarge their perspective on the world. There were lots more questions than there were answers, and much of what we had ingested as "the whole truth" was up for grabs.

Learning is a value we both still embrace, and yet "seeing what is right in front of us" (like this apple, in all its gloriously complex simplicity) is a skill we both continue to work on. Over the long course of our lives, we have both been in places where really "seeing" was the last thing we wanted to do, it seemed so much easier to just go along with whatever was transpiring. But as with most self-deceptions, sooner or later we usually saw the light. At that point, we would turn to one another to bounce around the perceptions, emotions, and possible courses of action emerging from our attempt to learn as much about ourselves and the world as we could handle at any given time.

We are also still working on the notion of what happens when one friend sees a situation differently than the other, we struggle to this day with how honest to be with each other, how to offer conflicting ideas with respect, when to speak up and when to hold back. When does concern for a friend become paternalistic versus helpful, how much input is appropriate, and should you offer it when it is not requested? Something that Bonnie does in her friendships has struck me as an elegantly simple way to address this problem. When I launch into a dilemma that I am currently experiencing, she usually listens without comment. When I have finished venting, she will ask "Do you want some feedback here?" To my surprise I have learned that although I usually do, there are times when I really don't want her comments or interpretations. Sometimes I just need to let it fly!

If all this sounds too "therapy-like" let me state upfront that we are both strong believers in psychotherapy and have availed ourselves of it at various points in our lives. However

we also both appreciate that sometimes the best therapy is to be heard with compassion and respect by a friend you trust with your life. To this day we are fine tuning the ways in which we can be upfront and honest with each other, and still respect the more fragile aspects of ourselves that can be sensitive at times.

To paraphrase that 90's rock song: we cry, we learn, we talk, we learn, we laugh, we learn, we love, we learn, and if we are both very lucky, the learning won't ever stop.

MARSH GRASSES

OIL BAR   **16″ X 20″**

I painted this piece after a death in my family and an illness. Capturing the flashes of light and bright color that occur in the dark, murky areas of marsh grasses reminds me of life cycles. Birth/death, happy/sad, light/dark; life constantly changes and opposites beg for integration in our lives.

G R I E F

This is the one that you just can't dodge. Yes, you may be able to deny anger, ward off jealousy, sidestep disappointment, and tap dance with guilt. But be assured that in the end, you will have to deal with grief. And if you don't do it directly, you can bet that you'll be doing it indirectly, in many ways and on many days of your life.

Bonnie and I grew up in Boston in a culture that was profoundly religious, largely repressed, and definitely not into the spontaneous expression of emotion, especially those of a painful nature. On the positive side of this ledger were rituals, often beautiful ones at that. They were filled with heart swelling music, mystical chanting, and the smells of incense and starched altar linens, mingled with the richly waxed old wood of gothic churches. I remember early on sitting hypnotized in a pew, the rustling of prayer book pages, the low murmur of responding voices, and the flickering lights of candles all transporting me to some other place where God was in charge and I was empty of all concerns, content to just sit and be present. Although too young to name it at the time, I believe that those moments tapped into the kind of inner peace that being focused and calm can bring, the deep richness of being awake and aware.

On the less helpful side of rigidly traditional religious instruction was the notion that there was a "right"

and a "wrong" in every situation, that things were either black or white and shades of gray were to be viewed with distrust – usually representing some attempt to reconcile something most probably sinful.

I share this as prelude to dealing with grief because in my own view, so much of what we bring to the table in any new situation has its roots in that old one where we gathered round as children. And what leaves us more naked and raw and heart achingly vulnerable than loss- and the grief that it so inevitably brings to us all?

My first memory of seeing my father cry was the day that President John F. Kennedy was murdered in November of 1963. I had just become a teenager and this tragedy that riveted our country marked an end to a period of innocence in my life and in the larger world. The shock and pain, etched on faces both in the streets and across the world via the television screen, were overwhelming at the time. As a country, we celebrated the rituals of the funeral with the Kennedy family, we shared their anguish and heartbreak and I remember thinking at the time that nothing will ever hurt this much again.

Fast forward a dozen years to my own departure from Boston with my new son to join my husband in Texas, and the news from my father that the cancer that we all hoped he had so gallantly beaten had in fact metastized, and that his prognosis was grim. Even as my gentle father shared this devastating news, he reassured me that my place was with my family and he would be just fine. Though my body flew away, my heart refused to budge, and it would take months after my father had died to align my grieving psyche with my new physical reality. I will never forget the pain of those months; indeed even today I feel a wave of sweet sadness recalling the loss of this giant in my life, whose strength and grace in such difficult circumstances were such a model for my family.

In the ensuing decades, losses have mounted and multiplied for Bonnie and me; parents, grandparents, beloved aunts and uncles, friends, and even the unspeakably sad loss of babies in our extended families. We have wept alone and together over some of these events and we still struggle with some of the grief that comes up for each of us when we face yet another loss. When my mother died suddenly eleven years ago, I called Bonnie to tell her the news. I was only able to choke out basic information before my words gave way to sobs and I heard in my friend's voice the echo of my own heartbreak. "Syl, I'm on my way." It was what I needed to hear.

And it was only two years ago, while at a conference in Keystone, Colorado, I was moved suddenly in midday to call Bonnie and share with her the exhilaration of my mountain "high". As I perched on a balcony five floors up and three fourths of a country away, contemplating the pine covered mountains directly in front of me, I dialed my friend. Although I knew her Mom had been seriously ill for months, I had no conscious notion in that moment that anything had changed. But as soon as I heard Bonnie's voice, I knew that her mother had died. It happened a few days earlier and she had been trying to reach me at home.

So as I sat in that glorious spot, we talked and cried and reminisced a little about her mother and the hole that her death would leave in our world. We had both now reluctantly joined that fraternity of those who have bid goodbye to the people who brought them to this planet. We also shared a good laugh about the funeral arrangements. Although distanced from it in her later years, her mom had requested that she be buried from the old Italian Catholic church of her childhood with all the ritual it entailed. Always at her best with an audience, Bonnie's mother Fanny never missed out on a celebration if she could help it.

If we have learned anything at all about grief over all these years, it is that it must have its own time and place. Grief has as many different faces as people, and what may be consoling and healing to one person may feel trite and perfunctory to another. In the best sense our grief is a way of honoring the being we have lost. It is our own personal tribute to the richness of a presence and a life that made a difference to us. It is one of the most profound, noble and wrenching human experiences that we can share. And it can be both exquisitely painful and joyfully celebratory. It is no accident that Irish wakes contain both funny toasts and fierce tears. Or that little old Italian ladies turn out for all the funerals at the church, previous acquaintance of the deceased is not required.

Acknowledging and mourning losses in many areas of life is part of the price of awareness. Not all griefs are about death, ask any parent who has just closed the door behind their last departing child. Leaving a once satisfying marriage, closing up one's home, even completing a major personal goal - they all have the potential to trigger sadness. Perhaps we defend against acknowledging some of our losses because we feel at times that they could overwhelm us. But so often, we misjudge ourselves and overestimate our fragility.

Like the marsh grasses in this painting, our grief has roots and blades that alternately deepen and wither away. Our grief may change colors and texture and transform its shape over time. And like all things in nature, energy expended is never wasted but recycled into something purer and simpler. The many tiny shoots of grief that we encounter in daily life form the foundation for our ability to handle the tough, sharp griefs that rip and tear at the very heart of our being.

Paul Simon sings that "Losing love is like a window in your heart." Sometimes the view from these new windows can offer some surprising vistas. Just when we think our world cannot sustain the latest loss we must bear, we glimpse yet another horizon.

And as for my thirteen year old observation that nothing in my life would ever hurt as much again – I couldn't have been more wrong.

Or more grateful.

CAPE COD SENTRY

ACRYLIC 18″ X 24″

One of my favorite walking routes takes me by this dead tree, which captivates me. While painting its twisted branches that reach for the sky, I was struck by it as a metaphor for aging. Although it has lost its abundance of leaves, it stands regally and without apology – creating this beautiful sculpture.

A G I N G

The old saw about aging not being for the faint-hearted rings increasingly true for Bonnie and me. We are less than two years apart in age and having made it through the fabulous forties; we are now engaged in finding out all that the fifth decade of life holds- that is besides more wrinkles, less agility, and lots of unfinished business in just about every corner of our worlds. In your fifties, the idea of standing alone becomes increasingly plausible as children make their final exit. (unless of course, they return!)

You find yourself and your significant other having long conversations about your HDL/LDL ratio, and may discover all your exotic body scents being overpowered by the aroma of those achy muscle preparations. Good shoes become your sacred quest and rather than worry about having dazzlingly white teeth, just having them becomes a priority. For all of us, body images and body parts have been altered by time and perhaps even by surgery. What we once considered our birthright: excellent eyesight, keen hearing, limitless energy, the capacity to recall somebody's name effortlessly, begin to declare themselves as the amazing gifts they really are. And, if we are at all aware (and some of us have much more trouble with this than others) some inner knowing reassures us that our lives really don't depend on clear,

unlined skin and cellulite free thighs.

Once this truth begins to seep in, possibilities open up. Rather than viewing the physical signs of aging only in terms of decline and disintegration, we can begin to appreciate them in the way we see the tree in this painting. Yes, our leaves may be gone, and our outer glory may be waning but a closer inspection may reveal a structure and substance that up to this point in our lives may have been camouflaged. Limbs that once proudly reached to the skies may now be slightly bent, and our bark may be scarred, but the stark strength of the foundation that has supported us and taken our lives through their different seasons is now becoming much more obvious to the naked eye.

As painful as it may be to our vanity, this shift also offers us some satisfying ways in which to regard others in our own forest. For those of us who have sheltered saplings, we now watch as they begin to grow in earnest, branching out in both expected and surprising ways, our years of feeding, pruning, and watering now supporting that skyward stretch. They grow beyond us and we exult as we wave them on. And those trees with thinning trunks and more fragile crowns appear lower on the horizon, as they begin that downward dance back towards the sweet cool earth that supported and nourished them in earlier days. Aging is about continuing, and in nature's rhythm, change and renewal are the constants.

When Bonnie paints, she has to squint often to get perspective on the piece she is working on, and as she points out, she is busily etching deep lines into her forehead and the area between her eyes. In today's quick fix and age–phobic world, a shot of Botulinum toxin would neatly resolve that issue but the result (much more difficulty with squinting!) would impact her creative work in a negative way. So wise woman that she is, she elects to accept the wrinkling, indeed to honor it as a sign of her commitment to the work that she loves. In fact the urgency in her life these days is less about retaining her physical beauty, and much more about optimizing her overall health so she can continue to evolve as an artist and as a person.

We have had many discussions over the past few years about the inner gifts that getting older confers. Lowering perfectionist standards becomes a necessity as both energy levels and the constricting idea of trying to live up to everyone else's expectations begin to head south. For traditionally raised women and notorious people-pleasers, taking time for the things we deem critical is enormously freeing. And once we start to wake up to the incredible brevity of our time here, it becomes less important to succeed and much more critical to just try!

Sharing our art, singing in public, standing up for ourselves in relationships all seem easier as we accept that it really is now or never, and opportunities require our action.

Bonnie and I are now moving towards that "sentry" position that aging implies. We have both lost almost all of our parent's generation, and the legacy of our families of origin now resides with us and our siblings. For our children and younger friends and family, we need to be mindful of the way in which we present aging, being honest about the hard things but also allowing ourselves to be downright exhilarated about some of its benefits. Although I still lose any consciousness of my chronological age while singing in public, and Bonnie still looks fabulous in her leather skirt, the fact remains that we are growing older and one day (we hope in the very distant future) we will let go of this life.

And one of the very basic joys of sharing a long friendship is knowing that although our youth was glorious and gone too quickly, mid-life is turning out to hold more depth, richness, and bare-bones intimacy than we ever imagined.

As for true old age, (which gets redefined for us all the time) we can only hope to get there together. We both strongly suspect that if current trends prevail, we have a good shot.

We recently shared a moment that hinted at what might lie ahead. While together a few months back, we ventured out walking to a local bookstore, bundled up against the cold wind. When we arrived at the store the heat inside triggered hot flashes for both of us and we wound up sitting outside sipping hot coffee while mopping our sweating faces. As we sat, two women, perhaps twenty years our seniors, passed by and looked at us with concern. "Aren't you girls cold?" they inquired. "No," we reassured them as we waved them on their way, laughing about the fact that the fires lit by menopause can so easily be forgotten. Obviously these two healthy, well-groomed, women on the go had transcended those sweaty moments and had gone on to other agendas. And some of it involved being out walking, exploring book stores and enjoying the winter sunshine. As we watched them trot off, chatting and enjoying each other's company, Bonnie and I decided.

We want to be just like them when we grow up!

TAKING TURNS

ACRYLIC   38" X 25"

Working on this painting made me think about the give and take between different colors. The larger yellow shapes move in a circular fashion around the darker colors, which move in and out of the yellow. Through taking turns, these colors reveal that they are multifaceted - dark/light, warm/cool, bright/dull. Each of the colors generously allows the other to speak.

GENEROSITY

"C'mon, it's my turn," protests the small girl being buffeted by the crush of bodies surging to mount the play equipment. Her plea is ignored as the other children clamber on the apparatus, oblivious to the tears now trailing down to her chin. Watching this little scene play out at a local playground, I am reminded of how critical it is to master this concept – the art of first claiming, then taking, your turn.

From my perspective, the middle child in a group of nine siblings, taking turns was as natural to me as breathing. From lining up for baths, waiting for your shift at the dinner table, getting a window seat in the car, it was all about recognizing that there were many bodies competing for scarce resources and learning to negotiate and compromise were vital to getting your needs met. Of course, fighting and the use of force were also a means to this end but in a family where boys outnumbered girls, and violence was definitely frowned upon, we tended to go for alternate strategies.

Our early training in the notion of give and take has parallels in the context of driving. We have all had the experience of slowing down in the right lane of the freeway to let a driver into the flow of traffic. In most cases the driver entering appreciates, accelerates, and joins the stream. In another scenario, a driver may zoom in at the last minute, forcing us to brake to avert a collision, and perhaps leaving us uttering some choice expletives. In contrast, another driver may hang back, hesitant and uncertain about when to go, again upsetting the flow of traffic and trying our generous impulse. Both cases represent an imbalance and it seems to me, generosity, and specifically this practice of taking turns, can serve as a counterweight to imbalances that exist in all areas of life.

I have been so lucky in my life to be surrounded by generous people. My spouse, renowned in our little universe for both his taste and sensitivity in selecting gifts, has rubbed off on my son and daughter. My son chooses elegant, thoughtful presents, and recently my daughter spent what was surely way too much of her first full-time salary on an original piece of artwork that will be treasured as much for the giver as for the gift. To my delight, they both have learned from personal experience that being as generous as you can provides far more happiness and satisfaction to the giver than to the recipient.

I remember being ahead of my son once on a busy Chicago street. He was a law student on a tight budget and I was on a business trip, taking him to dinner. Glancing back to see where he was, my eye just caught him bent over a disheveled older man sitting on the sidewalk as he slipped a few dollars in his hand. And anytime we would visit my daughter at college the word would go out that dinner was at her house, and she would trot us off to the grocery store to buy the ingredients for a community meal. The spirit of the gathering far outshone the quality of the food and to this day, she continues to gather new people into her outstretched arms.

But their most generous gifts to me are not made of anything solid. My son describing via email his impressions of Europe, his later blog of an extended Asian trip, my daughter's three page letter, left behind when she departed home for that final time, this generous sharing of their inner selves is what forms the absolute core of our relationships.

My friend Susan has filled my home with creative and cherished objects over the years, but much more significantly, she was my generous and constant "co-mother" when we both had babies and no extended family in the vicinity. Taking turns with providing timeouts for each other, and teaming up for holiday celebrations and marking family milestones enriched our lives, both individually and collectively.

Generosity can take surprising turns. I am privileged to know a writing teacher who exemplifies generosity in her skillful handling of a group of writers of differing levels of expertise. Jane greets each piece with a fresh eye and an enthusiasm that infects the class and helps us all to become better readers as well as writers. Jane's genius for helping people take turns is at least as valuable as her writing ability. And it makes being her student a profoundly enriching experience.

When I look at this painting and see the broad sunny regions that circle around the darker areas, it reminds me of the power of generosity to burrow through some of our outer layers into the less well lit corners of our hearts and souls. So often when we meet rudeness, impatience, or arrogance, we are tempted to respond in kind. Or perhaps for many of us, we are more likely to shut down and not respond at all. But when we can draw deeply on that most generous part of ourselves, we have an antidote to the depersonalization that so pervades our hurry-up culture.

Looking past some negative behaviors to the underlying imbalances that might be triggering them can be instructive. I have never failed to be impressed by the good-natured responses of certain employees of retail and food establishments when they are accosted on every side by demanding and sometimes obnoxious patrons. I have seen them greet what can be politely called "poor" behavior and turn the encounter totally around with their kind, calm manner.

Whatever these hardy souls have in their DNA needs to be isolated and then reconstituted and implanted in those folks who sometimes resist the concept that they too, must wait their turn.

Giving up our seat on the train to someone who is obviously in need, allowing that harried Mom with the petulant two year old to go ahead of us in the grocery store, volunteering to drive our neighbor to that doctor's appointment, all help us to exercise our more generous natures. My son was in the area of Ground Zero on 9/11, and recounted to me the absolute outpouring of New Yorkers in the aftermath of that hideous event. He was so moved by the offers to his fellow citizens of everything from food to shoes, to hoses to wash off the soot and dust as they made their way back home that day. In those searing days, the shine of human generosity pierced that billowing black smoke and ultimately made the unbearable somehow bearable.

And we must not forget the flip side of being generous, that is stepping up and taking our turn. For women, particularly those of our generation, this can be a challenge of enormous proportions. Women are known to defer when it comes their turn, to find all kinds of reasons why they shouldn't take that trip, earn that next degree, apply for that promotion, consider a major move. They are needed at home, they don't want to "rock the boat", their husbands might not like it. Taking our turn can be terrifying to some of us, perhaps turning us in a direction away from the sunny part of this painting into those areas that suggest something darker and more challenging. We may have to confront ourselves in ways that cause us to move away from our comfort zone and into unfamiliar terrain, but then again, isn't that what we have been doing for others all our lives? And don't we deserve to apply those same generous impulses, so freely shared with others, toward our own growth and happiness? Just as giving what is not ours to give causes imbalance in our lives, so does not ever getting what it is we truly want.

Bonnie recently made a decision that took her out of a comfort zone and turned out to offer an experience that contained far more bliss than angst. She received, from an unexpected quarter, a solo ticket to Paris. As a lifelong practitioner of the art of generosity, she was a bit taken aback and unsure of what to do as recipient of this generous gesture. So after some mulling, she decided to take the trip alone and enjoy it. Which she did completely, losing herself for hours in museums, dining alone at neighborhood cafes, and glorying in her ability to savor and relax as a tourist on her own terms. When she related her experiences to me, I was jubilant at her decision to step up and choose to take this journey.

It's definitely her turn.

IMPROVISATION

OIL BAR   **9″ X 12″**

I painted this piece during a time of turmoil in my life. Changing relationships, a bout of illness, the fierceness of some of the feelings triggered by these challenges are evident on this canvas. Colors and textures are jagged and raw.

A N G E R

It can be as subtle as a slight tightening of the jaw or fully declare itself in a marked physical shift. Often linked to hatred, it may also be deeply tied to love. For some of us it's tucked away in a place that's emotionally "off limits". For others it's as familiar and accessible as a smile. Just as its spontaneous eruption can be toxic and even deadly, so its controlled expression can be cleansing and transformative.

Of course the subject is anger- that much maligned, often feared, and thoroughly misunderstood emotion which "good girls" are taught to deny, and "tough guys" are encouraged to display. Just like this painting, done during a tumultuous period in Bonnie's life, anger has its own texture and tones. This canvas feels raw with its slashing strokes and bold colors. Looking at it reminds me of some of the metaphors we use to express anger: boiling mad, simmering resentment, cold fury, blinding rage.

What is so evocative both about this canvas and anger, itself, are their complicated presentation. Just as the black strokes here cover some other tones, so our anger can camouflage so much: shame, guilt, fear, grief, the powerlessness that may be triggered by a perceived attack or imminent loss. Figuring out what to "do" with our anger when it shows up (and for some of us, even considering the possibility that we might be angry!) means doing some serious mental legwork about its sources. We can all relate to that anger triggered by pure injustice, such as when we witness the unprovoked assault of a vulnerable person. In situations like this, taking swift action on behalf of the victim is entirely appropriate.

But often in our own lives, things are not all that clear. And when we find ourselves angry without any serious provocation, it's appropriate to consider whether we are having some kind of knee-jerk reaction, cleverly employed to prevent us from having to delve too deeply into its source, or perhaps using anger as our suit of armor, to keep us from further hurt in a seemingly hostile world.

For Bonnie and me and (I would bet my house) for many of our female peers, expressing anger in healthy, productive ways is an ongoing challenge. Between the two of us, we have covered most of the bases in sublimating our angry feelings via over-scheduling, overeating, sleeping too much or too little, numbing out, deferring, and saying "yes" with our lips, when our guts and hearts were screaming "no". A burning stomach, recurrent sinus infections, who knows if they are linked to unacknowledged hurt and anger?

Our more recent discovery is the power of that spark of anger to be used in service to ourselves and others. And if we can just wait out that first flare, allowing our anger to percolate, then settle in us, we have a shot at distilling it; draining off the bitterness and hurt, and letting it become the vehicle that we ride from that place where we definitely don't want to be, to a new and better destination. One of the great gifts of our anger, after reflection and understanding, is the clarity it can provide. For some of us, the point at which we say, "No more," marks a glorious turning point in our own personal history. And for a certain weary bus passenger named Rosa Parks in the 1950's, her individual decision of "No more," sparked a movement that would deal a major blow to the odious practice of segregation and change this country's history.

My daughter has the good fortune to work with a woman who, after experiencing a grave injustice affecting her child, turned a mother's rage (a force never to be underestimated) into political and community action. She created an agency that roots out environmental injustices targeted at the most vulnerable, and provides citizens with advocacy and a real voice in issues affecting them. Her transformed anger creates deep connections and widening participation in her community, and is a shining example of answering disrespect and disenfranchisement with resounding strength.

Another role model for me in the directed power of anger is the person I face over coffee each morning. My husband's childhood was marked by discrimination of the most perplexing kind- that based on ethnicity. His elementary years, spent learning in a language he did not understand when he entered school, were often filled with humiliation, degradation and the soul bruising burden of low expectations. The pain of that time still lives in some measure in the deeper corners of his heart and soul. Luckily, he also encountered a nurturing and wise teacher early on, one of those gentle souls who may never fully realize the contribution they have made to a young life.

Yet his life has always been, and continues to be about hope and joy and possibility. He has overcome, transcended, and celebrated and just by being himself has shined a light upon the fear and prejudice that close minds and hearts, and along the way has given many an opportunity to see things with fresh eyes. His commitment to himself, his family, and the community he seeks to enrich is the antidote to the hurt and despair that drove many of his classmates to simply drop out. The channeled anger of those damaged by systemic prejudice has always been a compelling force for social change.

This struggle to redirect anger and not turn it in on oneself is not unique to him. In fact when I look at people who have been the targets of oppression and disrespect and exploitation, I am often amazed not by their anger, but by their patience, their pride and dignity, their ability to keep their eyes on a larger goal and not give into displays of hostility. I know adult victims of child abuse who now mentor children, people who suffer grave physical disability and continue with a full life, some who have sustained tragic losses in their families but still build lives of richness and depth. Rather than retreating into anger, they march back into the fray and resolutely claim the good things in life.

As for dealing with daily annoyances: traffic congestion, mistakes in restaurants, people being late, we may want to ask ourselves if the situation we confront is really deserving of our anger. Depending on our level of arousal, some of these things can provoke reactions in us which may be wildly disproportionate. In my experience the more any of us regard ourselves as the center of the universe, around whom all things should flow smoothly, the more opportunities we will encounter daily to get angry about things not going our way. Do we really want to dissipate the power of righteous anger by throwing it away on the petty irritations of our days? Or could we choose to save it-then after serious self-examination to mobilize it's raw and sweeping power toward a more worthy and noble end?

So perhaps instead of swallowing, or wallowing, or unloading our anger inappropriately on an innocent bystander, we need to learn to welcome it in, to get comfortable with it in some fashion. Once we get past the first layer of our anger, we need to look deeply at the more subtle aspects. Just as this painting is loaded with undertones, so may that emotion we first feel as pure rage have elements of fear, or sorrow, or a longing for things to be different. We need to ferret out the root causes of our anger and allow ourselves to have the whole experience; just as when we look carefully at this canvas we can appreciate the whole palette.

Who knows? We may discover something that needs doing: a painting that needs painting, a story that needs telling, an injustice that needs to be confronted. The world is always longing to be made whole.

Using our rage in the process of re-creation may just be an idea worth trying.

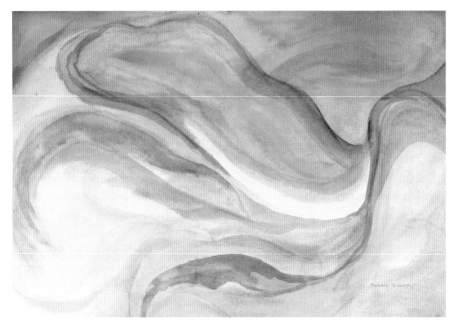

RAINBOW RHYTHM

WATERCOLOR   24" X 18"

My limited experience with watercolors encouraged me to flow with the medium and paint amorphic pastel ribbons of color on a blue ground.

SPONTANEITY

It began as an impulse. Wouldn't it be fun, proposed one of my eight siblings, to surprise Gay? Our "first" sister as we euphemistically call her would soon celebrate a milestone birthday, one which would be joyfully preceded by the birth of her first two grandchildren. Our extended family sprawls literally from coast to coast, so normally any gathering that includes us all must be planned in advance with the precision of a military strike. But this just felt different. The impulse raced around the country and without equivocation, we all signed on.

My sister's husband, consummate host and titular co-head of our clan, vowed that if we all showed up he would provide a feast worthy of the gathering, and began surreptitious negotiation with caterers for a full course gourmet meal, complete with pre-dinner cocktail reception. For a glorious few weeks, emails, whispered conversations, and discussions of a suitable gift flew across the land. Our sense of fun grew in proportion to our anticipation of my sister's face when we all showed up.

The execution proved as thrilling as the planning process. A number of us "kids" and my sister's son, a brand new dad, converged at her local airport on the Friday evening before the dinner. My youngest brother arrived last, striding towards us all with open arms and a few bottles of homemade wine. On the ride to her home, our excitement was palpable as we strategized ways to announce our arrival. We decided to hold aloft various portions of a sign reading "Gay, your birthday present has arrived." We pulled up in the early October evening cool and arrayed ourselves on the front lawn holding the sign over our faces. Like a mischievous school child, one of us raced to the doorbell, then scrambled back into formation.

A puzzled looking Gay and then her husband, Bob, appeared at the door. We beckoned her outside and as she struggled to read our sign in the gathering darkness, we lowered it and shouted a rousing "Happy Birthday!" A parade of expressions marched across her face; confusion, shock, incredulity, realization and then pure unadulterated joy. She literally trembled as she embraced her son, then all of us. The photos snapped of her in those moments are radiant with unexpected happiness.

The weekend continued apace with each new arrival eager to join the fun. Anecdotes competed with laughter as we unveiled our conspiracy. For the ensuing thirty six hours, we bore a temporary resemblance to a litter of puppies as we played together. We reminisced, wisecracked, caught up with one another and slipped easily into the roles we had played out almost half a century earlier. Left gloriously behind were our everyday lives with all the attendant worries about children, health problems, finances and the like. Leaving aside our political and personal differences, we gratefully climbed through the window of happiness this occasion opened up for us all, and just frolicked in the moment and in the warmth generated by our collective good will.

Late afternoon on Saturday brought an end to earlier rain showers and the sun emerged as if on cue when the photographer arrived for the group photos. Under the care of our host and the elegant caterers, we lingered outside in the waning sunshine. The wine flowed and spirits soared as we took our places around the table. The glassed in back porch of my sister's home became the most intimate of venues as we dined long and exceedingly well. It was an absolutely magical few hours, marked by toasts, tears, and bursts of laughter. In fact, the reality of the unfolding evening bore a striking resemblance to the one we had all pictured when the impulse to gather first surfaced. In the annals of our family lore, we were writing a new and tender chapter.

In retrospect there were a million reasons not to have this party. Not enough lead time, too expensive for everybody to travel, business and family concerns, any one of these variables could easily have short-circuited the evening. But the sheer spontaneity of the impulse, and our collective ability to see it coming to fruition, helped each of us to bypass all these practical objections in favor of something evanescent and inherently joyful. And once our energy beamed in that direction, its surge carried us seemingly effortlessly to this particular time and place.

On Sunday morning the dispersal began. Reality in the form of waiting spouses, young children, work obligations all surfaced again. But the glow from the previous evening softened the features of our middle-aged faces. As a group we were tired, happy, and inordinately grateful to have shared this time.

Our impulse, plucked from thin air, was now transformed into ribbons of happiness trailing us all back home.

MORNING LIGHT

ACRYLIC   24″ X 36″

In this painting, I attempted to capture the effect of the first light of the day. It bumps against the darkness and seeps through the cracks in solid objects, emanating a mystical quality.

COURAGE

I came across it accidentally while hunting for something else. Just a small piece of pink paper imprinted with the standard "WHILE YOU WERE OUT" telephone message. The kind that used to pile up on desks like litter on the highway, before voicemail, email and text messaging relegated them to the virtual dust bin. I remember glancing at it when I arrived at work one day and being struck by the words scrawled by one of our staff under the message line. "Mr. _____ called.

He wanted to say thank you for saving his wife's life yesterday."

Those who know me best would bust out laughing at the thought of me physically saving the life of any sentient being. As my adult children will attest, I am the one who ushers everyone inside at that first crack of summer lightning. I have no attraction to interplanetary travel, and unlike my daughter, jumping off high places into bodies of water is not my idea of an "awesome" time. When my son recently summitted on a Himalayan peak, I beseeched my prayer flags to flutter their pleas to heaven on his behalf, and some time ago, when my spouse recruited two of my brothers to join him on a climb to Mt. Rainier, I had to endure my mother's wrath in addition to my own altitudinal angst.

One of my more daring expeditions was a business trip I undertook to Lima, Peru in the 90's and the numerous cautionary tales told to me enroute by seasoned Limenos had elevated my blood pressure by the time we landed. But then again, being met at the airport, and then doted on all week by incredibly protective colleagues hardly proved worth the adrenaline rush. Mercifully, even the small earthquake that occurred in the night was tempered for me by both extreme jet lag and the fact that luckily, before retiring, I had consumed a therapeutic dose of the locally celebrated Pisco Sour.

My most recent encounter with a potentially dangerous situation came via an unexpected visitor at three o'clock in the morning while I was a guest in a Colorado condo. Having read on the road to Keystone that altitude shifts can trigger insomnia, I was dutifully tossing and turning on the couch with the nearby patio door open to the late night breezes. When I heard the noise of somebody entering the enclosed pool area directly outside this door, I tiptoed to the window to have a look. My brain had scarcely registered the rather imposing form of a large Momma Bear when I detected the much smaller form of her cub following about ten feet behind. As she approached to within about fifteen feet of where I stood, I ever so gently slid the door closed, then awakened my slumbering husband. He pulled on his pants (obviously a prerequisite for any bear fight) and we watched in heart pumping fascination as the pair ambled around the pool area, searching in vain for a snack, then reclimbed the ten foot fence into the night leaving us to our own wild speculations. After an animated conversation with our friendly innkeepers, we enjoyed the rest of that stay from a fifth floor suite.

So you are now asking, how would your average and decidedly non-swashbuckling worker like me rate such a dramatic phone message? My work takes place in a medical setting where we see lots of people in pain. Their pain is very real in its physical aspects and many patients have received less than optimal treatment for their disorders. And a large number of our patients have physical pain compounded by a more complicated kind. Often their spirits have been wounded almost to the breaking point, and one of these patients from a small central Texas town had recently spent time in our hospital program. She was at home again for awhile when the pain of her life overwhelmed her and impulsively, she decided to take an inordinate amount of medication and end her life. Luckily, she also decided to call the Clinic and talk with some of our staff. We were able to keep her on the line while we located her husband and the area paramedics, the genuine lifesavers in this story. After a timely trip to the hospital, all ended well, and it is my fervent hope that this person is glad to be alive today.

I saved that pink slip and when I catch sight of it now and then, it reminds me that buried in the most tedious, pedestrian details of our daily lives are opportunities to impact others in ways that may turn out to be profound. My eldest brother, long a hero of mine, has cared for a seriously ill family member with unfailing dedication, unflagging optimism, and uncommon courage. Somewhere inside him is a vast reservoir of grace that seems to replenish itself with each new challenge he encounters. As he laughingly reminds me, some days just getting up and out of bed is an act of courage.

Likewise, I bow to dear friends struggling with mental illness in their family, and to those with chronic financial hardship. Of course they get overwhelmed, but they somehow reach way down for that last scrap of hope to tide them over till their ebbing strength reverses flow, and carries them back to a place where they see daylight again. I marvel at the quiet dignity and determination of our parking garage attendant, an immigrant to this country, who juggles the indifference and occasional condescension of customers with a heavy load of college coursework to help achieve the professional job that will challenge his fine mind.

And finally, that pink slip reminds me that each one of us possesses the capacity for heroic activity. Most of us will not rise to the level of unstinting sacrifice that soldiers, fire-fighters, and other first responders routinely perform without regard for personal risk, and lucky for us, it's not required. Many everyday situations call for a different response and a conscious choice. Courage can involve seeing what is right in front of us, and deliberately and carefully attending to another human being in need. Sacrificing some momentary pleasure, comfort, or desire and giving of ourselves, even when we are not completely sure of the appropriate response, can be a kind of heroism all its own.

Yet keep in mind, that courage does not always require the affirmative.

For when we have given our best to a person or situation and it becomes obvious that our efforts are not helping, and even may be hindering the growth and development of another, finding the courage to say "no more" can be equally heroic.

Acting courageously in our relationships with others and the world can bring rewards that expand way beyond our initial effort. I recently spotted a greeting card in trendy gallery that proclaimed "while you may be one person to the whole world, you may be the whole world to one person". That boldly heroic notion may be worth recalling next time somebody in obvious need shows up in your world.

Saving lives is way beyond our reach most of the time. But practicing compassionate courage may bring depth and sweetness to our own.

MINIMALIST

ACRYLIC   10" X 13"

My goal was to make a succinct visual statement using very few strokes and a small proportion of bright colors.

Minimalist
SIMPLICITY

Less is more.

It's something that fine artists and writers know intuitively. As anyone who has ever walked along the Viet Nam memorial in Washington, DC can attest, the emotional resonance triggered by that ascending wall of stone is astonishing.

When Bonnie and I first met, I was attracted by her habit of buying classically tailored clothes. She sought out simple lines and good fabric, realizing early on that being seduced by the fashion du jour usually led to a closetful of obsolete garments come next season. It's a practice she still follows, and as I sit in her home writing these words, I am struck by the simplicity of her surroundings. Clean lines and neutral furnishings provide the backdrop for her paintings from which colors dance and dazzle the eye. Even her diet reflects the notion of embracing the basics; fresh fruits and vegetables abound while there is a total absence of "convenience foods"; a term which seems to suggest that cooking and eating are chores to be endured rather than two of life's great pleasures.

We are all alive in a time of prolific consumerism, when any and all human cravings can be translated into goods and services that are then marketed to us relentlessly from dawn right through the next one, via all of our encompassing technology. This steady drumbeat of the need to acquire more, do more and be more, underpins an increasing portion of our world and infects us all with an urgency that can confuse and obscure some of the more sacred aspects of our lives.

Weddings, births, significant birthdays, even high school proms now demand a protocol and cash outlay that stun people in less affluent societies. When my first child was born we brought him home to our attic apartment and a second hand crib, and an assortment of baby gear, both new and used, donated by relatives and friends. He lacked nothing vital and our ignorance of the subtle aspects of brain development led us to assume that everything he did was absolute genius.

With the advent of online registries, we now discover that Baby has a plethora of needs and luckily, the free market is eager to fill them. The same is true for wedding gifts, birthdays, bah mitzvahs, funerals and anything that occurs in between. In fact it is now possible to point and click our way through most of life's major touchstones without ever leaving the comfort of our chair. Especially with the gift registries, our job now is to move the merchandise, with gift wrapping and printed sentiments all handled for us by an anonymous third party.

I cannot deny the convenience of this commerce, nor having been both user and grateful recipient on occasion. The more troublesome aspect of the registry scenario is when the recipient calls all the shots. In this universe of neatly recorded preferences, what becomes of the endearingly tacky velvet painting, or quirky little clock, given for reasons special to the giver, that later get woven into the folklore of our lives? If all my gifts are pre-chosen by me, what happens to that little gasp of wonder when I open a box to find something I would never dream of asking for but am so delighted to receive? In shutting down unplanned giving in pursuit of efficient consumption, I wonder if we somehow impoverish the experience of receiving.

Similarly complicating are the fruits of being in constant communication. As the onetime parent of teenagers driving alone in cars, I fully appreciate the miracle of the cell phone. But the unstated ramification of carrying it is that you are always "on call". Missing a phone call is no longer just another roll of the dice but is evolving into some kind of imagined affront to the caller. And even as aging eyes and less than nimble fingers fumble with ever tinier buttons, the techno divide between early and late adapters is about more than just agility. Some of us claim private time and space beyond cell phone and text messaging as our birthright. Being in touch, both internally and with our loved ones, sometimes demands that we deliberately leave behind all those other needs that constantly call to us. And the gnawing anxiety about what we may be "missing" when we temporarily opt out of the technocracy, can be a force undermining our ability to just simply be.

For the younger members of our tribes, the dizzying array of choices in all areas can compound an already challenging time of life. Some of my nieces and nephews are currently engaged in the college decision. The competition to woo and win bright students is now on a level similar to large corporations. The pressure on these young people to make the "right" choice is absurd – surely an 18 year old has a lifetime of decisions ahead, some of which may be brilliant, and some decidedly less so.

From choosing which toothpaste will most whiten our teeth to which of the hundreds of channels we wish to watch on television, the constant exclusion of numerous alternatives may leave us keyed up and restless. The tyranny of so many choices can sometimes propel us back to the dilemma of toddlerhood. Witness in any commercial establishment the frustrated weeping of those small bodies surrounded by goodies, who want so desperately to have it all.

But before chucking our rampant materialism for a monastery in Tibet, a little common sense is in order. And as my son recently confirmed via an email photo from a Himalayan mountain peak, his sherpa guide's first act upon summitting was to flip open his cell phone. So much for the simplicity and innocence of ancient cultures. And I for one, am not willing to give up the amazing access to knowledge, resources, and communication afforded by some of our grown up toys.

Perhaps a few less drastic steps can ease us out of the "having it all" mentality and towards a more simple life. More attention to real needs for ourselves and for others, less attention to all those wants. More reflective thought when making decisions and less agonizing later about the alternatives we didn't choose. More discernment about what is really worthy of our time, efforts and resources, less chasing after every trend or fad that dominate our culture.

More or less? It's our call.

ABSTRACT SEASCAPE

OIL   **20" X 26"**

Wide horizontal bands of subdued color indicate the essence of an abstracted landscape free of human intrusion.

SOLITUDE

It can vary enormously from person to person. Some of us proceed happily through days filled with people, work meetings, conversation, and clamor and are never aware of a need to break from constant contact with others. For others, one overbooked day of appointments, obligations, and full engagement in all our modes of instant communication is enough to trigger a deep longing for the sounds of silence. Bonnie and I place ourselves squarely in the second group. Each of us has always craved our "alone" time.

And just as our need for solitude varies wildly, so do the places we seek it. For some it's that solitary stroll in the woods, my spouse retreats into his music room and the world beyond those walls falls away. An empty church with flickering candles encourages a state of reflection, while my daughter used to climb up and perch on the roof of our home to do some of her "heavy thinking".

This abstract seascape points us toward a time honored spot for solitary contemplation. Its dreamy quality invites us to cast our eyes outward and for me, awakens memories of a ritual from my childhood.

Our house was urban, its saving grace the curve of blue water clearly visible from the front steps. On every sunny day and many cloudy ones, my mother marched a column of us down the street and onto that beach. My mother, her sculpted cheekbones set off by her trademark chignon, had brown-black eyes, and favored tiny gold hoop earrings. She wore a ruffled sundress over her bathing suit. With escaping tendrils of hair blown around her face by the sea breeze, she exuded an appeal that made passing eyes linger.

The best beach days were when she swam with us. A former lifeguard, having her undivided attention during a swimming lesson was pure luxury. First you floated on your back until she flipped you over, her hands under your midsection. She would call the beat for your legs, "Kick, kick, kick." Then she would show you how to make oars with your hands to slice through the water. Throughout you held onto her delicious sturdiness and implored her not to let go yet. She never did. In fact sometimes you had to remind her. "Let go, Mom, I'm ready." And slowly, a little reluctantly, she did.

Then after settling the group of us up on the sand, confined to our blanket with the oldest in charge, she would cover her black hair with a white rubber bathing cap. We would follow her with our eyes to the ocean's edge, where she would lean down and splash herself to lessen the shock of entry. Then she would stride out and dive, disappearing beneath the waves. Just as our hearts froze within us, she would break the surface and emerge like some joyful sea creature loosed from an underground cave. She would bob her white head in our direction, flash us a thumbs up and start her swim.

And swim she did, with fluidity and grace that made her a cinch to spot in the water. Her long, lazy crawl kept her body low and straight, and the slow turning of her face as she came up for breath rendered her a ballerina of the sea. She swam steadily, heading out to the open ocean. She had told us on many occasions that France lay on the other side of that ocean, and we halfway suspected that she might be heading there without us. Alone, out there in the water she radiated freedom. The message telegraphed to our little tribe back on shore came from a being that was more than just our mother, and the solitude of her private ocean imbued her with grace and a seemingly magical power.

Just at the moment that the distance between us threatened to become unbearable, the pull of our longing created a magnetic field. The diminishing figure would execute a slow circular turn and begin the swim back to shore. She would emerge from the water shimmering in the sun, snatch off her cap and towel herself off, even as the littlest ones lifted their arms to hers. And the older among us would somehow know that she had traveled to places we could not then really fathom, but once again, she had returned to us.

Looking back I realize now that these swims were probably the linchpins of my mother's sanity, tiny blips of freedom in a life filled to bursting with the care and feeding of others. The gifts of her swims were those of solitude; a refreshing time-out, an internal spaciousness, and literally, a chance to float momentarily and slip the bonds of responsibility that connected her so deeply to us.

And now, in a time when an astronaut can cast his ballot by email from somewhere in the heavens, the pursuit of solitude offers an enormous challenge. Our televisions, computers, pagers, and cell phones seduce us, creating the illusion that we are "in touch" when in fact, much of what happens in these modes of communication is hurried and truncated. And even when we decide to turn them off, they worry us about the edges of consciousness, leaving us to wonder if we are "missing something". Indeed we may be missing something – the opportunity to communicate with the person most critical to our lives, our very own selves.

Technological wizardry, constant communication and busyness carry a price. And if all those voices in our ears drown out the sound of our inner voice, then it seems a poor bargain. Cultivating the practice of solitude, refining the art of spending time alone is an act of courage. Getting to interior spaces that are as bare and uncomplicated as this stretch of beach is vital for both physical health and emotional integrity. And knowing how to operate the most complicated computer program is no triumph – if we are strangers to the software of our own hearts and souls.

Finding the off switch in our daily lives can be first step to locating the source of our real power.

SEASONAL DANCE

ACRYLIC   16" X 20"

I started this painting on location. It began as a representational painting of a small scrub pine surrounded by marsh grass. Back in my studio, I realized the painting did not render the life that was in the actual scene. I abstracted the painting and it became a seasonal dance.

REINVENTION

At the moment I am a living paradox. A woman who looks longingly at the salt and pepper hair and make-up free, gloriously etched faces of my friends, and then completely caves in the face of a male stylist. He suggests a lively auburn shade, even touching up my eyebrows in the process and reassures me I will look "terrific".

This particular field trip is to an upscale salon, one which caters to women who call home at intervals to speak in halting Spanish to their maids, while regally accepting the icy goblets of lemon water served to them by the attentive shampoo staff. As I lean back over the shampoo bowl, my neighbor chats on a cell phone and completes her luncheon plans allowing that she is "famished", I wonder if the older woman shampooing her hair feels the same way.

I am at the salon today courtesy of my spouse, the man who delights in giving experiential gifts; a full body massage, a night in a fine hotel. He gets great pleasure from pampering those in his orbit, a lovely trait in a partner.

Slightly problematic for me is that I am not as comfortable in the pampering situation as the women around me appear to be. My stylist asks me what I have in mind and I am forced to confess that I have no master plan. My hair is fine, not nearly as thick as it used to be, and is fading fast as the latest boxed coloring

job has worn its way through a number of shampoos. He runs his hands through it, flipping it around as he advises against highlights. Wrong, he decrees, for my level of curl. He pulls me from the chair and marches me off to see the shade of auburn he is proposing, resplendent on the head of one of his colleagues. Given that she is at least a dozen years younger and has a few more pounds of hair, I am momentarily doubtful.

But buoyed by his optimism and take charge demeanor I squelch my doubts, and just sit back as he paints my scalp with his magic potions. This is the part of the experience that I enjoy – the talk about where he grew up, the serious bout with illness he recently had, and some of the alternative medical treatments he is pursuing. My stylist is turning out to be a smart, savvy guy with an enormous reservoir of good humor. He tells me about his home remodeling experiences, we chat about restaurants, and I feel cozy and relaxed within his little cocoon. As we talk, women flow by us, blown dry women with luxurious manes of highlighted hair. I glimpse a stunning Asian woman with a few magenta highlights and a perky blonde with bangs, whose hair bounces as she trots across the marble floor.

I am ready, he announces, to go sit under the heat for awhile. I sit and relax under the warmth of the dryer's circulating fan, taking my place in the line of ladies who rely on the twin goddesses of cosmetics and high end hair care products to help achieve their most glorious selves. After another few rounds of washing and rinsing, I don a thick white towel and adjourn to the sunlit center of the salon to again await the magic hands of my stylist. Feeling more a part of things, I amble out to the lobby and pour myself a cup of steaming coffee from the silver urn. The plate of cookies beside it looks relatively untouched, and as I glance around I realize most of the women in here look like they haven't eaten a cookie in at least a decade. It dawns on me that the notion that you are tempted but don't indulge is part of the training, an exercise in self-control for those who take their skin and hair seriously. So for the moment I ignore my growling tummy and coolly pass them by.

Finally I am summoned back to the cubicle of my own Henry Higgins, the man who assures me that my guy will definitely notice the changes in me this evening. Momentarily, he looks alarmed. "He's not a real uptight guy, is he?" Absolutely not, I reassure him, for a middle-aged man he's as hip as they come. He brightens and proceeds with the untoweling. Although my glasses are off, I get a distinct blur of redness, similar to the jolt you might get from a vivid non-objective painting, colors that exist only in an alternative reality. That sense begins to creep up from my shoes as I view my new red head. As I look in the mirror, I realize the expression I found puzzling on the woman I just greeted in the Ladies room was probably horror when she saw the color of my eyebrows. I am now wearing that very same look.

Oblivious to my inner turmoil, my stylist continues to comb, cut, and sculpt my hair. As he coaxes and spritzes, I plot my escape route. Luckily, things are dull at the office and I can proceed straight home to commence the seventy five washings it will take to tone down my smashing new color. Breezily, my stylist assures me that after a shampoo or two I will look "totally natural". Sure I think as my red eyebrows dance madly back at me from the mirror, natural for a recent graduate of clown college.

After honing every hair on my head to Peter Pan length, my stylist rubs gel on his hands and constructs a do that is some amalgam of Sharon Osbourne meets Lucille Ball. This seems to satisfy his deepest creative urges and at that point, he pronounces me done.

"I think you look amazing," he announces. Wordlessly, I have to agree. He then beams at me with such pleasure that it thaws my paralysis and moves me deeply. After all, I gave myself over to his creative genius, and in his eyes I am far better for it – and definitely far redder for it!

The fact that I now resemble a punked out Julie Andrews really is not his fault.

After all, what did I really expect? When my mother was my age, she wore her long gray hair pulled back in a chignon. If only I had inherited her cheekbones, I might have followed suit. I try to imagine her reaction to my new and happening look, and strongly suspect that she is enjoying a major laugh from the next world. She was never much for salons either.

As I generously tip the valet (he is a perfect gentleman about keeping a straight face) and pull into the traffic, I get a glimpse of myself in full daylight. And then the whole adventure begins to seem ridiculously funny. And I acknowledge to myself that even in my middle age, spas and salons are not places where I will ever feel inherently at home. All that attention to hair and face is lovely, but for me, and I suspect for a number of my peers, it's just not who we are. This latest foray into the world of relentless and pricey self-improvement confirms that although you may still win a battle, any war against the absolute reality of growing older will ultimately be lost. And just what is this search for cosmetic salvation all about anyway? When does a healthy interest in one's appearance spiral into a consuming preoccupation which obscures the inner richness and deepening beauty that aging gracefully can confer. There is absolutely nothing wrong with coloring your hair and caring for your skin, but doesn't the condition of our minds, hearts, and souls deserve at least equal billing?

So perhaps it's time for me to stop admiring salt and pepper heads and let nature begin to take her course. The people in my life who simply acknowledge their age but live on their own terms, while caring with love and humor for their aging bodies, are by far the most intriguing. All food for thought. And speaking of food, one decision taken this day is irrevocable.

If I ever do revisit that salon, I am definitely having one of those cookies.

BACKLIT

OIL   20" X 26"

I was moved by the light behind the solid tree trunks. These opposites seem to balance one another.

INTEGRITY

My earliest memory of being part of a public demonstration dates to when as a uniform-clad twelve year old, I marched in a hometown Thanksgiving Day parade. "Keep Christ in Christmas" read our human chain of letter-carrying children. I was the "C" in Christ. The Irish and Italian Catholics lining the route cheered madly at the spectacle of their scrubbed and perky foot soldiers, all happily secure on the side of the Almighty.

My next forays into the areas of social justice were a bit more nuanced. Bonnie and I came of age in a college mecca in the early 70's – there was always a demonstration underway. Civil rights, anti-war protests, women's rights, it was a dizzying and volatile time in our lives and in our country. I was bred of parents who believed passionately in the dignity and worth of individuals. They also insisted that violence was never the answer and that violating the law, even in the service of a higher good, was risky business. Thus, I developed an uneasy truce with myself in the arena of public protests. I attended a few, at least one with Bonnie where we sang, clapped, and rallied. But when the police showed up – and they always did- I moved along. Although I admired those willing to risk jail for their beliefs, I drew the line at custody.

So, in the recent past, when my then college-aged daughter called to say that she was on her way to the United States Army School of the Americas (a facility in Georgia where US troops have trained Central and Latin American soldiers) to participate in a protest, it touched off a mind wave for me. Lots of conflicting thoughts, an equal array of emotions. She would ride a bus for two days and camp out along the way. She would have to decide whether to cross a line into the facility and risk arrest for trespassing – in this case a federal offense punishable by up to six months in jail. Her intention was not confrontation, she told me, but rather to be present.

"If you knew what happened when these soldiers returned to their countries, the innocent people who have been murdered, you would be there too."

Even as I supported her willingness to stand for her convictions, I worried about possible consequences. She promised to think about it. And she did, long and hard on the trip down. And when she arrived and joined in the procession entering the facility, she found her answer. She crossed the line holding aloft the name of a person who had been killed in Central America. When they called the roll of names, she answered, "Presente."

There were a number of people arrested that day but my daughter was not among them. When the soldiers invited them to leave, she quietly filed out. When she related all this later, I was struck by her manner in the telling of it. Unlike the sometimes circus-like atmosphere of some of the marches and rallies I had attended as a young person, there was a powerful sense that in participating in this action, she had crossed a line into new territory. A place where each one of us holds some responsibility for the world we share. Where purposeful, profound silence can challenge the mighty roar of authority. A place where in speaking somebody else's name, we find our own voice.

As I remember these events and look carefully at this painting, I see reflected in these bare and sturdy trunks, the same kind of silent but potent witness that emanates from people acting out of their integrity. Just as these trunks sink deep into the soil, and then reach for the sky, so our integrity both roots us and allows us to grow and stretch in the service of living out our core beliefs. Like the bark on these trees, our integrity both protects and exposes us to the surrounding world. And the ways in which we grow, bend, and weather events in our lives are intimately linked to the values we embrace, and the ways in which we integrate them in our words and actions.

Both my daughter and I have marched again in peaceful protests since that day. And Bonnie and I continue to talk at length about the increasing urgency we both feel about living lives that outwardly resonate with our inner beliefs. From choices as simple as the kind of foods we eat, the kinds of things we acquire, to the kind of work we pursue, there will always be competing realities and priorities. When we find ourselves in conflict about our choices, it is vital to examine our "first principles". So often what appears to be a problem is really an unwillingness to be very clear with ourselves or with others. Living with integrity requires a level of honesty that can push us to our limits.

But, as these trees so eloquently remind us; it's a noble, worthy quest.

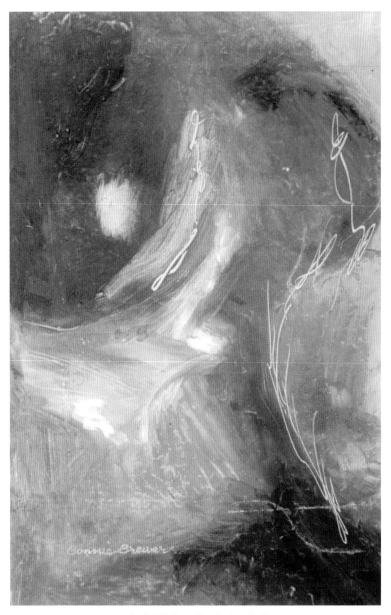

CAVE DANCE

OIL BAR   14″ X 18″

The gestures of my paintbrush on this canvas led me to the feeling of a figure dancing joyfully on the wall of an ancient cave.

J O Y

It surfaced shortly after we met. We weren't innocents after all; obviously we both had a past. We told each other bits and pieces, testing the waters. Then the plunge into full disclosure: the cold hard fact that we had each done a stint in a rock and roll band.

My then husband-to–be had played bass guitar. I, absent any ability to play an instrument, was a vocalist. At the tender age of nineteen, with long curly hair, a good tan, and a few beers to overcome my extreme self-consciousness, I could belt out tunes for hours on end. Although my band mostly practiced (and I enjoyed a brief but soulful romance with the blond, philosophy-majoring bass player) my experience was short but sweet. My husband had the more impressive resume, having played for a number of Catholic school dances on his local circuit. He had even been paid in actual cash.

After marriage, graduate school, work, and of course, children, took over our lives, with the exception of an occasional session with the acoustic guitar, our brief musical flings were forgotten.

Until my husband's fiftieth birthday party, that is. Having recently emptied our nest, we decided to celebrate the event in grand style. As a nod to our new free agency status, I delegated to my younger brother (another guitar-loving man) the task of buying a shiny new electric job for my spouse.

The party was a smashing success. The seductive red guitar was "sweet" and with it, the musical floodgates switched to the ON position. Additional guitars, drum pads, amplifiers, sound systems and mikes began proliferating at an alarming rate in our son's former bedroom. Since midlife bands don't usually have gorgeous young vocalists hanging out and soliciting them for work, I was pressed into service. Clutching my thirty year old tambourine in my hand, I began to actually enjoy our jam sessions. So when my mate proposed that my fiftieth birthday celebration include a band gig at a local dive at which I would get to sing a few songs, I signed on. Our guests, ranging from seasoned old rockers like us down to children, tore up the dance floor and appeared to have an all around terrific time. Left that evening with buzzing ears and hopelessly sore feet from dancing in my heels, I was hooked once again.

One thing led to another and a few months later I found myself en route to a large auditorium full of my husband's coworkers for a midday gig. I was shot through with a mix of excitement and stage fright which was producing heart zapping bursts of adrenaline. Luckily my daughter was serving as roadie/chauffeur. As I confided my growing angst, she took me firmly in hand.

"Relax, Mom. Nobody really cares how old you are, what you look like, or even how well you sing. If you get up there and just have fun, people will have a good time right along with you. So just sing your heart out."

What a sage. Just as she predicted when the music began, my nerves vanished and as we entertained the crowd, amazing things started to happen. People rose, clapped and sang along, and actually began to dance in the aisles. My husband (ever the showman!) had drafted folks to loose large beach balls into the gathering, and as we played the old tunes, gray heads were bobbing and arms were reaching up all over the theatre to keep the balls moving through the air. The hour and a half we had been allotted passed way too quickly. At the end of our set, I was slated to sing a slow song that demanded strong vocals. In practice I had been hesitant about committing to sing it, not sure that I was ready for the spotlight. But nodding to our drummer, who really liked the song and wanted very much to play it, I took a deep breath and plunged ahead. Although I'm sure it was quite unremarkable to anybody in the audience, I know I will not forget that next three minutes for as long as I draw breath. Embracing my daughter's words, I simply stood there and sang my heart out, and in exchange I received little nuggets of pure joy. Moving through the audience after that performance was surreal with people offering kind words and compliments. But the joy that I felt that day was not only about the reception that our performance elicited. Most of it was a result of that loss of self that happens when you totally give yourself over to something else. In losing my self-consciousness and suspending the relentless activity of comparison and evaluation, I allowed myself the luxury of full presence. It was like tumbling through a secret passage into another place.

Almost without exception, this has been our experience with every other gig since that day. When you give yourself fully and freely to making music for people, they respond in very visceral ways. And the joy that we have experienced in our crazy little band is unique to each, yet also shared among all. So many times we have grumbled at practice, constrained by time, or fatigue, or job pressures that can make getting together arduous. Yet when we settle in and start playing, we can surprise ourselves. An improvised and skilled solo here, a notable improvement in an old standard there; it leads us once again to that place of unexpected and pure happiness. In the hours we do practice (always longer than we plan, as a recent late night visit from a visibly amused but exceedingly polite young police officer can attest) we shed job responsibilities, family pressures, physical problems and the like.

We are just a group of people working together to produce something we can feel happy about and invariably, we do! For us children of the 50's, making music in our fifties has been a pure serendipity, a second chance to develop that part of ourselves that was necessarily submerged by early responsibilities.

Recently we pulled off what had been my husband's dream gig – staging a rock concert for the three generations of my family, and some long time friends who gathered at a Cape Cod resort. Billed as their opportunity to get in touch with their "inner rock stars", my family stepped up, with my brothers belting out their old favorites and my sisters teaming up for a few ballads. One nephew filled the room with his amazing blues as another took the drums for a solo. Even our son, who tends to view our band antics with amused detachment, got caught up in the moment. In-laws, cousins, even the new grandbabies took to the dance floor for the finale, and the sense of celebration and joy that spilled out of that room bound us together in ways that will be relived for decades to come.

I think the joy I felt that night was exceeded only by my husband's, who worked with superhuman zeal to coordinate and plan this event from 2,000 miles away. And as it turned out, he was right on target, it was all so worth it. My sister wrote a note thanking us for bringing the band as it was the catalyst, she noted, for all of us to just break loose and enjoy ourselves. She went on to say that "being in the moment" is the gift we all gave each other that night. And she pointed out, it gave the next generation something to hang onto (not to mention to mock us with unmercifully) for years to come.

As we recently recalled the glory of this evening in a late night conversation, I reminded my husband of one of the other aspects of band life that seems to break in our favor.

In my band incarnations, the bass player always gets the girl.

BAY VIEW FROM PORCH

WATERCOLOR   14" X 18"

After a trip to Nantucket in June, I painted this from a photo of a
rose-covered house in Siasconset, Nantucket.

COMPROMISE

It began as one of the happiest days of her life- the marriage of her fourth son and ninth child, and her final appearance as parent of one of the principals. And just as for the previous eight, my mother was primed and ready to go on what turned out to be an extraordinarily hot day on the mid-Atlantic coast.

Having enthusiastically celebrated my parent's July 4th wedding anniversary until my dad's death in 1976, my family was particularly thrilled to have a new July union. We all gathered, twenty plus grandchildren in tow, to witness the vows of my brother and new sister-in-law. The ceremony was simple and lovely, made more endearing by the presence of a priest friend of my brother's and mine, who had met my mother on a number of occasions, when she visited our neck of the woods.

My mother seemed a bit subdued on the afternoon leading up to the wedding, but we chalked it up to the heat and the previous night's party. When following the church ceremony, she felt a little faint and asked for a chair, we were concerned but figured the air conditioned country club and some food would revive her. However after neither made her more comfortable and she grew increasingly pale, it became obvious to my sister, the nurse, and I that she was feeling no better. So we called and met the paramedics as discretely as possible in an adjoining room. Although my mom turned on her considerable charm for them, these earnest young men seemed to sense a potentially serious situation and insisted on transporting her to the local hospital. So with an honor guard of grandchildren waving and shouting "Bye, Nana!" my mother, wearing a slightly chagrined smile, was lifted into the back of the ambulance. She sent back a regal little wave from her sitting up position on the gurney. Her jade green silk dress made her face seem luminously white as she was driven slowly away, the vehicle's dome lights winking in the gathering darkness.

Twelve years later, the events that transpired that evening still seem surreal. My mother arrived, alert and responsive, at the Emergency Room and caused quite a stir as her tuxedo clad sons and dressed up daughters began to show up in force. The staff bent on trying to enforce the "immediate family only" rule was perplexed, then capitulated in the face of such numbers. While undergoing a CT scan, she experienced an "incident" which resulted in an immediate loss of consciousness. As we would discover later that evening, this incident was in fact a massive hemorrhagic stroke which instantly inflicted searing damage to critical parts of her brain. In the space of an instant, that burst blood vessel transformed my iron-willed mother into a strangely vulnerable looking, inert older woman, whose gray and white hair usually worn pinned up in a bun, now splayed over the pillow like dry seaweed on the sand. A ventilator, its hose taped around her mouth, emitted a steady whooshing noise as it pumped air in and out of her lungs. The medical staff told us that it was possible she could still hear us. Stunned and unbelieving, and gently pushed along by our priest friend, we visited her in pairs to deliver our tearful prayers and entreaties that she not succumb to the forces that seemed to be pulling her inexorably, right out of our orbit.

It was this sudden drama that would dominate the next five days. If my mother had one thing to which she gave primacy above all else in her life, it was her independence. She guarded it ferociously facing widowhood, major surgery, and her recent retirement with her own resources, always insisting she would do it "her way". Now the question for us was what would "her way" be in this situation? She had told some of us laughingly, that if we ever kept her alive past the time she could function fully that she would "haunt us". This night, none of us felt very much like laughing.

As one might imagine with nine adults, each of whom experienced parenting differently, there was a spectrum of reactions and opinions about how to handle this turn of events. A few siblings moved instinctively to the position that our mother would never choose to live like this and our obligation to her was crystal clear. Others were hesitant, reluctant to even voice such thoughts, and others still just overwhelmed at the knowledge that our mother's life now literally lay in our hands.

Over the next few days and with the help of some fine and deeply compassionate physicians, we entered into an emotional and profound dialogue about all of our own wants, needs, and desires versus those of our life-supported mother. But as time passed even the most emotionally attached of us came to accept that the final gift we could give our mother would have to be the most selfless one we ever delivered. For a woman who valued dignity, privacy, and mobility above all else, the prospect of being diapered and tube fed was absolutely out of the question. And gradually amid tears, hard questions, and gut wrenching sadness, we came to a consensus. We had to love her enough to direct the doctors to unhook the ventilator and let my mother, as she had done so unflinchingly throughout her life, once again call the shots.

We decided that the final outcome must be placed back in her own hands and if she strongly wished to live, she would do so. We also suspected that if she felt her sentient life was over and her mission accomplished, she might just choose to depart, leaving us (as my sister wistfully observed) always wanting more of her. We gathered for the extubation and prayed mightily that she would not die as soon as the machine was disconnected. In what would be her final maternal act, she did not. My sisters and I maintained a vigil whispering endearments, and thanking her for both her nobility and the fierce love she had bestowed upon us in life. And after about ten hours off the vent, she wound down and died peacefully with one of my brothers sitting by her side.

And in that whole period of her dying, so many grace notes. Deeply spiritual, my mother ended up in a Catholic hospital (the same one in which our new sister-in-law was born and her father was a faithful volunteer) and was anointed by our priest friend. She slipped away from us on the eve of her own wedding anniversary, celebrated fifty two years earlier. The staff of the hospital, much taken with our story, was tender and respectful. And my mother, ever impressed with savvy medical professionals, was attended by a neurosurgeon who was both smart and very handsome. That would have pleased her enormously.

We buried her back home, one week to the day after my brother's wedding, some of us wearing the same clothes we had packed for the first occasion. Another simple and elegant service marked by my eldest brother's moving eulogy and our faces mirroring for one another the pain and shock of that week. As we all struggled to integrate the loss of our matriarch, it occurred to me that the past seven days, containing both lovely beginning and poignant ending, had perfectly distilled two of the central tasks involved in living conscious, grateful lives.

Loving each other with all we have, and when it's time, letting go.

AUTUMN ABSTRACT

ACRYLIC   16" X 20"

Painting on location during the fall was bittersweet. This was my attempt to capture the last shout of brilliant color before these trees undressed for their winter dormancy.

R I T U A L

I have walked way more than a mile in my mother's shoes.

In fact, the navy blue size 7AA Ferragamos I inherited after her sudden death were hands down the best pieces of leather I ever tied around my feet. I wore them till the soles were thin and depleted and after years of devoted service, I reluctantly laid them to rest. I wish I could have kept those shoes forever.

Luckily I inherited many other things, most of which are non material and surely as imprinted in my DNA as the short waist and slim ankles that we share. A precious part of my psychic inheritance is a sense of ritual and celebration.

Some of this is owed to growing up Catholic in a city where there was a church on every corner. May processions, Easter vigils, Christmas pageants, and the like dominated our early years and each and every liturgical celebration meant a corresponding one at home. First communions brought parties with aunts and uncles, complete with cake and ice cream, while Easter usually meant an after church stroll for the eleven of us through the Boston Gardens, stiff but proud in our fine new clothes.

In addition to rituals that grew from religious traditions, we had a number of family traditions that developed over the years. My father had a position for a number of years where he was required to work late on Wednesday evenings. My eldest sister was in charge, as my mother worked evenings to help meet the financial needs of raising nine children. So my dad figured out a way to both keep us in line and reward us for doing homework and the dishes, while not doing each other any permanent bodily harm. When he left work and took the subway home, he would always stop at the corner store and pick up a gallon of ice cream and a few bottles of soda. When he arrived, he would unload the bag and we would set to work mixing ourselves root beer floats, ice cream sodas, or if it were a particularly festive night, hot fudge sundaes. He would sit and listen to all our news of the day as we prepared his treat, and in this little circle of contented, ice cream smeared faces, there was conversation and relaxation. Although today's dietary gurus would frown on eating sweets that close to bedtime, my father was wise enough to understand the power of celebratory foods to foster a sense of warmth and family closeness. And he ensured that after a long day at the office, he would get the most enthusiastic of greetings!

In addition to the fun rituals, my family of origin had its share of the less pleasing ones. Many a Saturday morning my dad would awaken us to the stirring strains of the "Saber Dances" played at near max volume on his beloved German stereo.

As we struggled to consciousness (the teenaged members of the family cursing under their breath) we would begin to straggle downstairs. My mother would have pancakes or some such breakfast and then the tasks of the day would be assigned. Dusting, vacuuming, waxing furniture, polishing silver, laundry, endless errands – there was so much work to be done given the number of people housed under our roof. I remember as a child wishing mightily that I could just goof off on Saturday like my friends.

Later as the mother of only two children, I cannot imagine how my mother faced yet another weekend of cleaning, cooking, and attending to the needs of so many people. And a holiday, a party for guests, a dinner gathering brought special tasks. Ironing the linen tablecloths, polishing up the good glasses, digging out the silver chest and setting the table, all were closely supervised by my mother, whose attention to detail surpassed any drill sergeant's. Before an event she would be in a frenzy of planning, cooking, and preparation, leaving us all breathless and wishing we were elsewhere. But she always pulled it off – the flowers were perfect, the table inviting, and guests invariably raved about my mother's flair for entertaining. I vowed when I grew up I would NEVER get that intense about hosting and in general, I don't.

But I must confess (and I am sure my children will attest) I absorbed some level of that sense of ceremony my mother had when entertaining. For the first thirty years of our marriage, we owned no formal dining room set or china. My husband and I married in the early 70's, while still college students and our informal, low key wedding did not encourage this type of legacy gift. So we made do, and had many a satisfying gathering with our mismatched but colorful dishes, and it was my ongoing challenge to pull off a formal dinner. A few years ago, when my friend Fran and I went shopping with her bride-to-be daughter, we happened on a sale of bone china that was simply too good to pass up. So without much forethought, I signed on the dotted line to become the proud owner of service for eight with a number of complementary serving dishes.

When the boxes arrived a few days later, I unpacked them with a strong sense of déjà vu. As I examined the understated pattern and held a plate up to the light to view its translucence, I could almost feel my mother's appraising glance over my shoulder. And it dawned on me that this acquisition and the pure satisfaction I felt while placing them piece by piece in my china cabinet, were a direct link back to her. I may have established and enjoyed my own style in entertaining, yet some part of me had remained unfulfilled. In my purchase of china, and of course new flatware to use with them, I was closing a circle. And inside of it I felt connected and content.

When my daughter was young, she would ask me why I was singing when I was occupied in doing things around the house. As a teenager, she asked in a considerably different way, strongly suggesting that I cease such annoying activity immediately, and most urgently not do it while driving her around with friends. So it was a particularly sweet discovery, when visiting her home a while back, to hear her crooning away as she moved around her kitchen doing her daily tasks. She told me later in that visit that her friends comment, often favorably, on her tendency to hum and sing as she works. And I strongly suspect that like me with the dishes, she sees this as evidence of a deep imprint of the life we once shared under the same roof.

Back when my husband was an avid runner, he would set out his gear on Saturday nights for an early morning extended run on Sundays. Gone long before the rest of us rose, he would revel at being out and active in the clean cool quiet of the morning. On his way home he would stop for bagels, delivering them to us with a face flushed and shining from his morning ritual. We greeted him (and the fresh bagels) with pleasure.

In my own family we also share, like all families, many rituals around the celebration of Christmas. We have always been suckers for enormous Christmas trees, usually ones that involve both sawing and swear-ing as we wrestle our trophy into the house. This immediate past Christmas, my husband and daughter were taking a pre-Christmas trip to Mexico and my son was flying in from an extended trip to Asia just days before the holiday. This left me to set up and decorate the tree, a task I truly love.

But as I was working solo this year, I decided not to drag down every box from the attic and showed some restraint in decorating our smaller-than-usual tree. We had a good reunion when everybody arrived and as we were preparing for our Christmas eve open house I noticed my daughter scanning the ornaments on the tree.

"Hey Mom." Ever so casually. "Didn't you put all the ornaments on the tree this year?"

No, I allowed. And I asked her which particular ornament she was missing.

She mentioned a pair of ornaments that had been given to us twenty five years earlier by our then elderly neighbors. They were gold-plated and engraved with the children's names and over the years they had grown tarnished. Though I had seen them in the box, I had not hung them this year, focusing instead on some of the newer, shinier ornaments we had acquired in recent years. But as I watched my daughter's face, I was reminded once again of the power of traditions and rituals and the source of comfort and continuity they provide.

Although she is a highly functional independent woman in everyday life, in the calm and slowed down fullness of Christmas eve, a part of her is once again a child looking forward to the celebration of another holiday, and looking back at the touchstones and the tokens of her past. And her life will not always allow her to spend her holiday with us.

I left the room and didn't return until I located the missing ornaments. She didn't say too much when they reappeared on the tree that evening.

And that is perhaps the central and saving grace of our shared rituals. At their best they bind us and remind us of what we hold precious and in common. We get to make them, we get to break them, and in a world filled with activity and assaulted by noise, they speak for themselves.

WARRIOR 1

<u>ACRYLIC</u>   31" X 25"

The gestures of the objects in this still life reminded me of a strong warrior mounted on his horse with his sword and shield.

TRIUMPH

It's such an evocative word. Just saying it aloud conjures visions of knights on a sacred quest or a brilliant researcher shouting "Aha!" as she straightens up from her microscope. Victory laps, gold medals, the aviators' thumbs up – all celebratory gestures.

At life's beginnings, one triumph seems to lead naturally to another in a round robin of milestones. The baby learns to walk and home and family are forever changed. One of my daughter's early triumphs sticks in my memory – a day when after playing outside in the yard she burst into the kitchen, brown eyes blazing. "I did it Mom, I did all the monkey bars," her small self exulted. After trying for weeks she finally mastered hand over hand and the moment was thrilling for both of us. The first school experiences bring lots of opportunities for small victories in everything from academics to sports.

Simple tasks mastered by children yield to more complex challenges in young adult life; leaving home, choosing a course of study, that first job. The pure joy in my son's voice when he was granted admission to the law school of his choice is something recalled to this day. We rejoiced that his hard work had resulted in this realization of a goal he had set for himself.

All kinds of accomplishments can bedazzle us as we mature into our lives. Landing that plum position, being recognized for an outstanding performance, achieving athletic prowess, and pursuing our artistic and creative goals can all lead to triumphs, both small and stunning.

But then a funny thing happens as we get along the path. The triumphs that beckoned so seductively when we were starting out begin to lose some of their shine. What may have been blind pursuit of goals is now tempered by a realization of their costs. And with time and maturity, the glow of individual achievment may yield to a growing longing for connection and community.

Given this ripening awareness of both the brevity of our lives and the softening of goal driven behavior, we may become a bit more selective about our heart's desires. My husband strove mightily towards his goal of completing a marathon in what he considered a "respectable" time. After many months of training, three stress fractures, and a shot of cortisone in his aching foot from his sympathetic physician, he did finish it in regulation time in the year he turned fifty. An amazing feat? No. A hard won triumph? Absolutely.

Our definition of triumph may well expand to include all kinds of choices which may have seemed suspect just a decade or so ago. A friend's decision to step back from some administrative responsibilities to focus more on his teaching, which in turn affords him the opportunity to care for his grandson one day a week, is a tender victory both for him and his impressionable new sidekick. A young professional's decision to abandon the world of high finance to enter the classroom and change the world, can have life altering consequences for both this teacher and the students. Deciding to put career driven energy into volunteer work for a non-profit can be a brilliant choice. And recently, I attended a show by two artist friends who then proceeded to give away most of their work to those of us lucky enough to be present. As they told their friends and colleagues, their lives together contained more than they had ever dreamed and they were now showing their work from a position of abundance, which left them feeling they could freely give their art. We all left that gathering sharing on many levels in their joint triumph.

An extraordinary person in our extended family faced one of life's most searing tragedies, losing her beloved mate to a disease that caused him to take his own life. Standing together at her wedding to another good and loving man five years later was an occasion of pure happiness for us, and a powerful reminder of life's ability to turn those hours of lead back into gold.

As we encounter more of the variables of life's endgame, like illness, reduction in status and income, and the loss of illusions about what our lives might have been, opportunities to triumph abound. Our children can throw us curves that leave us breathless and we can wall off from problems and deny them, or gather the courage to search for the common ground and mutual respect necessary for our relationships to thrive. A creative project or unfulfilled dream that has lain dormant for decades may surge to consciousness, and our willingness to step off the worn roads of our lives and try a brand new path can make us feel alive in ways we could not have imagined. Aging and all of its transforming circumstances will come to us all, and we have the option to meet them head on with determination and resolve, knowing fully that no amount of effort will forestall eventual senescence and death.

The triumphant path now seems less about specific victories and much more about remaining alive and open to the changing topography of our lives. And as we finally grow up and are able to excavate some of those lost and buried parts of ourselves, sifting through the dirt to uncover what may be precious, we can find much cause for rejoicing.

Awakening each day to the certain knowledge that our days are numbered and the world can and does break our hearts, presents us with an ongoing choice.

We can pull the covers up over our heads – or get up and on with the dance.

WHIRLWIND

OIL BAR   **16" X 20"**

I had fun layering the colors from my oil bars to see what would happen. I picked up a green oil bar and a red one and capriciously made marks on the top of this multilayered painting. Working spontaneously, I felt lighthearted and amused while doing this piece.

Those medical miracles just keep on piling up. We witness them on nightly newscasts, when we log on to the web, when we read our newspapers, and they boggle our minds with what is now possible in restoring and healing human bodies. Organs, digits, whole limbs are now transplanted in ways we could only have dreamed about a generation ago. And recently another milestone was passed with the first facial transplant-certainly a marvel that poses at least as many problems as it solves.

Yes, skilled surgeons can replace our corneas, our aching, worn-out knees, and they can swiftly re-contour those parts of our bodies that have developed that "lived in" look that is so unpopular these days. But as far as I know, not even the most brilliant medical talent has yet been able to transplant a sense of humor into a patient lacking that commodity. Indeed, a funny bone implant still seems a remote possibility.

From my perspective, a well functioning sense of humor is one of the more vital requirements for full humanity, and those among us who have this trait and spread it around for all to share give us an enormous gift. Anybody who has ever experienced a deep, gut busting belly laugh can verify this idea. Bonnie and I have never had to search too far to find something wildly amusing. And most of the time, it is our own behavior that will send us into fits of laughter.

My friend Fran, who was a communications major in college, wears her finely honed sense of humor like a comfortable backpack, using its contents to help her negotiate all kinds of life situations. She is both valued coworker and desirable party guest because one can always count on Fran to deliver a line that will leave people laughing. A memory of her that still elicits a chuckle is an entrance she made to a party at my home some years ago. As she came through the door, she greeted me in her normal voice which tends to carry.

"Hi – hey, do you think I have this dress on backwards?"

Conversation stopped as people sitting in the room looked up to check. And everyone within earshot burst out laughing at this tall, good natured newcomer whose dress, we decided, was definitely facing in the right direction. Another more recent Fran moment occurred at a local restaurant when we met to celebrate my husband's birthday. As she was running a little late and we were seated far way from the entrance, the whole dining room got to witness her striding across the room carrying a huge guitar-shaped plastic container of popcorn, adorned with Elvis Presley's picture, part of her gift to my guitar loving husband. A low ripple of laughter ran across the room as the other diners joined momentarily in the fun.

Both of these entrances highlight some of the finer aspects of good humor. Humor that is gentle connects rather than distances us, and heals rather than hurts. Self-directed humor often elicits the biggest laughs as it reminds us that despite all our posing and our artifice, we are all both human and deeply fallible. Moments that might be difficult, embarrassing, and potentially painful can be cleansed and transformed with an injection of healthy humor.

Back when my husband was in graduate school, I remember a dinner with one of his classmates, an African American man who had grown up in the projects on the East Coast. As he was relating some of the tales of his childhood, he began to laugh. When we asked him what was funny, he responded with a tale of his involvement with a local charitable organization. He and his elementary-aged school friends were asked to go out and collect clothes and household effects for a drive for the holidays. He got very excited about the project and said he was so pleased with all that his group was able to assemble. So, he told us, you can imagine my confusion when come the holiday, some of the very stuff we had collected came back to my house. Up until then, he noted ruefully, I had no idea that I lived in a "blighted slum" and my family was part of the "deserving poor"! What impressed me about the

way he painted this little scene were the self-deprecating tone and the genuine amusement with which he told the story. Choosing to see this mischaracterization of his life with humor, helped him defuse a humiliating and hurtful experience.

My sister and I had an experience in a restaurant in Carmel a few years ago that can make me laugh aloud to this day. We went to dinner at a very high end Italian restaurant which, on that evening, contained mostly couples enjoying romantic dinners. Sitting beside us was a long-legged and lovely young woman, who was dining with a significantly older man. My sister and I just happened to glance at her simultaneously, and at that very moment she tossed her head back, parting her lips seductively as she flirted with her date. We resumed eating and after a few moments this couple left. When I glanced up a few moments later at my mischievous sister, I nearly choked. She had just taken a healthy bite of her tomato caprese salad and as she caught my eye, she threw her head back and, opening her mouth, she arched her eyebrows at me suggestively. After a few glasses of water, we had recovered ourselves enough to finish the meal and we laughed all the way back to the hotel. Normally, making fun of somebody in a public place would not fall under my rubric of good humor. But my sister's tongue in cheek take off on a romantic moment in that idealized setting was hilarious in both its spontaneity and her physical expression, and no harm was done to our anonymous couple, who had already left the premises.

Not all humor is universal but the sense of fun it conveys can cross boundaries. My friend Nancy is a brilliant musicology professor, who lectures from time to time at our Museum of Fine Arts. At some of the lively and fascinating talks she has given, I have noticed her chuckling while introducing a piece of music, as she related some anecdote about the composer. On a few occasions she even laughed aloud, and although some of us in the audience missed some of the nuances of the joke, we laughed right along with her at her sheer delight in the subject matter. Such is the power of a witty and enthusiastic presentation – it can deflate some of the seriousness and pomposity often associated with academia and the fine arts, and open some space to breathe and relax while we try to absorb new concepts.

But humor, like all precious and powerful commodities, must also be handled with care. Vicious humor, ethnic and racial slurs, sexist and degrading jokes, can all cause damage that may leave permanent scars. While creative political satire can skewer the hypocrisy and inflated egos of some in public life, rabid personal attacks masquerading as humor do nothing to advance either side in a political debate. And rather than bridge a gap between people with opposing ideas, cruel and cutting humor effectively shuts off real debate and shuts down minds and hearts.

In our lives, humor has been a bulwark in difficult times, a bridge over deeply troubled waters, and a vehicle for transforming some painful situations, as well as a way to celebrate some of the downright funny moments of daily life. At its very best, humor can dissolve barriers and allow us to see each other as the vulnerable and lovable creatures that we truly are. Being able to sit back and laugh at ourselves helps liberate us from the relentless pursuit of our goal-driven lives, and can create the space for warmth and community among us.

And after working with people who have chronic pain for many years, I can honestly say that I haven't yet observed a face that does not look softer and more appealing when decked out in a genuine smile. Many times in training people in relaxation techniques, I will find them initially frustrated as they struggle to relax facial and jaw muscles that tend to stay locked in patterns of bracing and tensing. I will deliberately make a joke at this point to watch what happens with muscle tension levels as the person begins to laugh. Almost invariably, the muscle tension readings drop as the person "lets go" of trying to relax and the face softens into a smile. People are often astonished at the results and this empirical evidence only reinforces what we know to be true. Smiling, chuckling, giggling, and a good belly laugh are all excellent therapeutic techniques. And another point in their favor, there are no adverse side effects.

In a time of the aforementioned medical miracles and the increasing complexity of our daily lives, laughter may well turn out to be one of our most effective medicines. And in a time of out of control medical costs, one thing we can assert with absolute certainty.

It's the best bargain around.

AUTUMN LIGHT

ACRYLIC   **16" X 20"**

I painted from a photo of deciduous trees changing color in the fall.
I wanted to express the leaves exploding with their orange-yellow
color against an autumn sky.

FEAR

They had known each other only days and they were already taking their clothes off together. The cold metal lockers and sterile little cubicles stood in sharp contrast to the laughter and warm greetings of the women using them. And this day I joined them as Bonnie slipped into one of the dressing rooms to gown up for her stint on that cold table that stood behind the wall marked "Radiation Area" in large red letters.

This particular chapter in our friendship had begun about eight weeks earlier when I called Bonnie to wish her a happy birthday. Not wanting to worry her, I decided to downplay a biopsy that had just been scheduled by my doctor to check out something seen on an ultrasound. As I casually related this news I was stunned by Bonnie's reply.

"Well Syl," she began in an equally offhand tone. "Turns out I'm having a bit of a health challenge too. I have just been diagnosed with breast cancer."

Fear zapped me like an electric shock. As I struggled to match her calm tone we got through the initial details, the growth was very small, she was going to see an excellent surgeon in Boston, and all signs from her doctors were that this was the best case scenario, early detection and immediate surgery with follow up radiation. We talked awhile reassuring each other that all would be well

and when we hung up, I promptly burst into tears. The next two months, including Thanksgiving, Christmas, and New Year's passed in a blur of doctor visits, surgery, recuperation and reports as we entered this new territory. My results were absolutely fine and I think we both rejoiced that our energies could now be beamed towards restoring Bonnie to wholeness. Bonnie came through her surgery with her usual grace and aplomb intact and when she was ready to undergo her radiation, I was able to travel and join her for one of the final weeks of treatment.

I expected to find her haggard and pale, with very little energy for anything beyond daily trips to the hospital for her treatments. I should have known better! She was thinner but full of plans for long walks, lunches with friends, and her eyes had their usual sparkle. It was the middle of winter and Bonnie lived on a pond which afforded glorious views, with sunshine illuminating the snowy grounds and the ice crystals that hung from the low roofline. In that strangely cozy and consoling week, we had long and emotional conversations, many of them based around things like this illness that can trigger our most profound fears.

When you receive a diagnosis of cancer, Bonnie wryly pointed out, all those fears you have about "not being enough" can very quickly crystallize into a much more primitive one of "not being at all". Opening this new window on mortality in our lives prompted much discussion about fear and the ways it had impacted both of us. How many times, we asked each other had we held back, said "No," deferred, or simply not attempted something due to being afraid? And as we talked our way back to the roots of some of our fears, we found the same old bogeymen that haunt many of us from childhood. Fear of disapproval, of being alone, of not living up to expectations (our own and others), of failing, of succeeding. And in our continuing dialogue, we both realized that in our fifty plus years we had already encountered all these things. We have both been heartily disapproved of, one of us lives (quite happily!) alone, we have succeeded and we have failed and here we were, laughing about it all at Bonnie's table.

We decided that the most potentially devastating fear (and ironically the most simple to address) is the fear of fear itself. After all, with the exception of thrill-seekers, who likes those heart pumping, sweaty palmed, churning stomach feelings that can come when we attempt to do something out of our comfort zone? But what we forget (and people far wiser than us have counseled) is if we can just keep going through the fear and all its attendant discomfort, we get to make our way to the other side of fear, and the sweet and satisfying sense of accomplishment that comes when we pull off something we were not at all certain we could do. It's a high that trumps any achieved with drugs.

Since her bout with cancer, Bonnie has made some significant changes in her life, certainly not without real fear. But this brush with a potential killer has also emboldened her in many ways, and has clarified for her how she needs to spend her time and efforts. Her urgency to live as fully and deeply as she can has been intensified. When I called her the week after her radiation ended to find her making plans for a helicopter trip around Manhattan to shoot photographs with her artist friend, I knew she had crossed back into the land of the fully engaged.

Early last December, Bonnie called with the news that something suspicious had again been detected on her mammogram. As I was already planning a visit, I pushed it up to accompany her to a visit with her oncologist in Boston. A few nights before the scheduled appointment, we took a ride to the tip of Cape Cod to view the Christmas lights and have dinner. Riding along in the wintry dark, Bonnie launched into a topic that went right to the bull's-eye of my fear.

"I just don't want all that stuff, Sully," she began in a normal conversational tone. "You know I watched my dad with all those treatments and if I am that sick, not able to paint or enjoy life, and I'm just going to die in the end anyway, I'd just as soon skip it."

I listened in silence, glad for the inky black of the roads.

"You know Syl, I just want to live out my life as happily and well as I can and just be grateful for all that I have had. And I really don't want anything very formal at the end, OK? You know what I love, good food, some wine, some really great jazz, just a big party for the people I loved. Nothing too heavy duty, you know that's just not my style."

My heart contracted as I searched for my normal voice. Here was my lifelong friend offering me this profound gift, laying out, calmly and clearly, what might be the final tasks of our long and incredibly rich relationship. I struggled to quell the fear and loss that rose in me at the thought of losing this person so central to my life. But this moment was not about my fear, rather it was about fulfilling the deeper requirements of being a friend. After a moment I managed to exhale, and responded that I would honor all of her requests and decisions just as I knew she would honor mine. And added a silent but fervent plea that I would not be tested anytime soon!

A few mornings later we headed to Boston and the oncologist in a sudden snowstorm that made the roads both lovely and treacherous. We made the clinic just in time and soon enough I sat alone in the waiting room, with just the hiss of the heating system and the pounding of my own heart to keep me company. After a while, a very pale and markedly thin young mother entered with her husband and three small children. As I contemplated what lay ahead for them this holiday season, tears stung my eyes.

And then Bonnie, radiant and smiling. False alarm, whatever was on that x-ray had been there all along, no changes, no new growth. We celebrated by walking a mile in snow and blustery winds to the Museum, where we feasted and celebrated the most blessed of glad tidings, a clean bill of health.

As we reveled in this latest reprieve, I told Bonnie about a pamphlet I had spotted in the clinic as she checked out at the desk.

"Well-behaved women don't make history," proclaimed the cover.

Neither, we both suspect, do fear filled ones.

EARTH QUILT

ACRYLIC   16" X 20"

Painting for the first time after being diagnosed with breast cancer, I began mixing dark colors on this canvas. This led me to reflect on the inevitability of death, as well as the sunlight that shines on the earth, germinating seeds which later manifest as flowers, vegetables and weeds.

WHOLENESS

We recognize it when we see it.

In some quiet and unassuming way, it declares itself. Maybe it's the quality of their presence. Something calming and reassuring emanates from these folks whether they are chairing a meeting, playing with their kids, or even sitting alone in a coffee shop. Without making a sound, people who possess a sense of themselves as whole persons telegraph volumes. And here lays the true paradox of genuine personal power.

It has taken Bonnie and I many years in our own lives to grasp that being a whole person does not necessarily involve executing multiple roles, varied professional experience, a complex web of relationships, or even a healthy bank account. Any of these things might help us uncover our wholeness but they are not related to it in any significant way. In fact they sometimes can be an impediment. Promotions don't make us whole, a dream home doesn't do it, and neither do exciting friends, public acclaim or even around the world travel. And even our most sacred acts—marriage, childbearing—don't guarantee our wholeness.

Because wholeness is not a goal to be sought after with endless striving and superhuman effort. Rather it is our birthright, our natural state, as central to each of us as our eyes, our smiles, and the individual beating of our own hearts. We may come to this place tiny and helpless, but we are also very much whole when we arrive.

And for so many of us this wholeness we possess as children comes under assault as we begin to grow up and experience our worlds. We are impacted profoundly by our family lives, educational systems, religious institutions, our cultural communities, and a myriad of influences bombarding us constantly with messages that may or may not be true. And then there are the messages within the message-unspoken and insidious-that whisper to us about what makes us valuable. All too often they tell us that our worth can be measured by the car we drive, the clothes we wear, the neighborhood in which we live, or the definition of our muscles.

For women alive today these messages can be particularly cruel as the bar gets raised, yet again, on physical appearance. Witness the growth of eating disorders among the very young, and the burgeoning practices of cosmetic surgeons everywhere. Another growth industry is the area of "anti-aging" medicine which features all kinds of potentially problematic "treatments" for the latest disease – one which we used to know as normal aging! In this time of Bonnie and I becoming older women, our wrinkles and the normal bodily changes that come with maturity are now being recast as shameful signs of self-neglect. And instead of accepting our changing physical appearance as the normal process of our lifespan as we "come of age", we are offered a full complement of medical and surgical procedures to help us look and feel as "youthful" as we possibly can. Even as my vanity thrills to the notion of retaining some vestige of fresh faced, eternal youth, I know in my soul this cannot be the path to wholeness.

Beyond the cosmetic wars, there are far more hurtful ways of destroying a sense of wholeness that are constantly operating in our society. From sharing a different skin tone, or eye shape, to worshipping a different god or having a different sexual orientation, the ways in which we label and then discriminate against those who don't meet "our standards" is soul killing, and inflicts damage on the perpetrators as well as their intended targets.

I have written throughout these essays about my husband, who has modeled resiliency for me in a way that has profoundly impacted my life. Growing up in this country as a second generation American, but as the child of low income migrant farm workers, he bore the twin indignities of being cut off from the Anglo mainstream culture, while also being discouraged from taking pride in his ancestral Mexican heritage.

About fifteen years ago, he had the opportunity to travel to Ireland as part of a government task force and while there, he wrote me a very moving letter about the enchanting warmth and welcome of the Irish. As I have not yet visited the home of my ancestors, his perspective was fascinating to me. Ten years later, I was asked to travel to Mexico City to conduct some training, and I invited my husband to accompany me to the capital city. Since we had only been to Mexican border towns, and coastal "tourist traps", he was quick to agree. As I watched him over that trip, absorbing some of the amazing history and culture of this huge metropolis, I sensed a kind of awakening.

Subsequent trips, both professional and personal, have fed his curiosity about the land of his grandparents and the more he learns and explores, the more his pride strengthens. Seeing with his own eyes the murals and wondrous museums of Mexico City, the Mayan ruins of the coast, and the art and architecture of the central mountain areas has exploded the lies this culture promulgates about Mexico and its citizens. He has been connected to the history and culture of his ancestors, and also to a deep source of healing and wonder in all that it contains. In a very real sense, accessing the reality of Mexico, and not just the racist stereotypes of his youth, has been a major step towards wholeness.

I recently attended a two day seminar on healing racism at which a film, featuring some graphic and heartbreaking accounts of abuse and degradation suffered by native Americans at residential schools in the United States and Canada, was shown. Many of these schools were staffed by missionaries, and their badly misguided efforts in concert with their governments to "kill the Indian, save the man" left searing wounds that cannot be undone. Films about the enslavement of African Americans and the consequences that haunt us to this day were equally disturbing. When we refuse to see the inherent beauty and value of other ethnic groups and their traditions, terrible things happen. And people broken by our harsh insistence on conformity at any price may spend the rest of their lives searching for a sense of wholeness, a place where they can belong and be at peace.

Listening to the stories people shared in that little cocoon, where they could trust enough to air some of the humiliating and wrenching encounters they had experienced, convinced me anew. For us all to feel whole, we truly need to see every individual and their respective culture as a valuable piece of our "earth quilt".

As Bonnie and I are increasingly aware, this search for wholeness can lead us many places– some appropriate and healing while others may be destructive dead ends. But ultimately the compass must swing back toward us, to our own true north, the place where we store up our joys and triumphs and our grief, shame, and sorrow. For it is the full spectrum of our lives that make us who we are. Rather than the numbers on the bathroom scale or the degrees that hang on our walls, it is the small stirrings in our souls that remind us we are precious and worthy of attention and respect. And even when our bodies might be ravaged and our lives contain more failures than successes, the pilot light of our wholeness is never completely extinguished. Rather it waits patiently for the opportunity to ignite once again, to nourish our true and finest selves.

These days Bonnie and I have arrived at a place in our lives when the barriers to wholeness are coming down. Expectations for both of us feel more realistic and comfortable, with a little more breathing room now than we felt as younger women. We are decidedly older, both physically and experientially. We are often happy, occasionally confused, and sometimes, profoundly sad. We still laugh together frequently but we are now also more willing to share our tears. And perhaps most satisfyingly, we can now reflect something for each other that was always there, but not always clear.

Despite any and all messages to the contrary: we are whole.

Each and every one of us.

Thank you for reading our book. We hope you found it a satisfying investment of your time. As mentioned on the dust jacket, one of our hopes is that readers can and will find some "common ground" in reading about some of the experiences we have shared, as well as some of the emotions and insights they have provoked. And if spending some time with this artwork brought up some dormant creative urges, get out those paints and let us know how it turns out!

Bonnie and I both believe deeply in the power of reflection and thoughtful conversation to help us uncover what is true for us in our lives.

This is not to suggest that we have any kind of lock on the truth – in fact you may find yourself in strong disagreement with us on various ideas presented in this book. For example the essay that explores the way in which my mother's life ended may provoke very different reactions in some readers, and in that case, we urge you to have a conversation about end of life issues with people you respect and trust. Similarly, a reader may feel that our observations about the need for simplicity are idealistic or irrelevant, and once more, we encourage you to explore that notion with whomever you would like.

Who knows – you may find yourself in a lively debate with any number of people and we are only too happy to imagine that you will jump in and take your turn! If this book can stimulate even a few colorful conversations about any topic, we rejoice in that possibility. And if you lack a conversational partner, please feel free to visit us at: www.conversationsincolor.net

You gave us your thoughtful attention.

We promise no less in return.

Sylvia and Bonnie